Cambridge Elements

Elements in World Englishes
edited by
Edgar W. Schneider
University of Regensburg

WORLD ENGLISHES AS COMPONENTS OF A COMPLEX DYNAMIC SYSTEM

Edgar W. Schneider
University of Regensburg

Shaftesbury Road, Cambridge CB2 8EA, United Kingdom

One Liberty Plaza, 20th Floor, New York, NY 10006, USA

477 Williamstown Road, Port Melbourne, VIC 3207, Australia

314–321, 3rd Floor, Plot 3, Splendor Forum, Jasola District Centre, New Delhi – 110025, India

103 Penang Road, #05–06/07, Visioncrest Commercial, Singapore 238467

Cambridge University Press is part of Cambridge University Press & Assessment, a department of the University of Cambridge.

We share the University's mission to contribute to society through the pursuit of education, learning and research at the highest international levels of excellence.

www.cambridge.org
Information on this title: www.cambridge.org/9781009663250

DOI: 10.1017/9781009289504

© Edgar W. Schneider 2025

This publication is in copyright. Subject to statutory exception and to the provisions of relevant collective licensing agreements, no reproduction of any part may take place without the written permission of Cambridge University Press & Assessment.

When citing this work, please include a reference to the DOI 10.1017/9781009289504

First published 2025

A catalogue record for this publication is available from the British Library

ISBN 978-1-009-66325-0 Hardback
ISBN 978-1-009-28948-1 Paperback
ISSN 2633-3309 (online)
ISSN 2633-3295 (print)

Cambridge University Press & Assessment has no responsibility for the persistence or accuracy of URLs for external or third-party internet websites referred to in this publication and does not guarantee that any content on such websites is, or will remain, accurate or appropriate.

For EU product safety concerns, contact us at Calle de José Abascal, 56, 1°, 28003 Madrid, Spain, or email eugpsr@cambridge.org

World Englishes as Components of a Complex Dynamic System

Elements in World Englishes

DOI: 10.1017/9781009289504
First published online: July 2025

Edgar W. Schneider
University of Regensburg

Author for correspondence: Edgar W. Schneider, edgar.schneider@ur.de

Abstract: This Element proposes to view World Englishes as components of an overarching Complex Dynamic System of Englishes, against the conventional view of regarding them as discrete, rule-governed, categorial systems. After outlining this basic idea and setting it off from mainstream linguistic theories, it introduces the theory of Complex Dynamic Systems and the main properties of such systems (systemness, complexity, perpetual dynamics, network relationships, the interplay of order and chaos, emergentism and self-organization, nonlinearity and fractals, and attractors), and surveys earlier applications to language. Usage-based linguistics and construction grammar are outlined as suitable frameworks to explain how the Complex Systems principles manifest themselves in linguistic reality. Many structural properties and examples from several World Englishes are presented to illustrate the manifestations of Complex Systems principles in specific features of World Englishes. Finally, the option of employing the NetLogo programming environment to simulate variety emergence via agent-based modeling is suggested.

Keywords: World Englishes, Complex Dynamic Systems, complexity, usage-based linguistics, construction grammar

© Edgar W. Schneider 2025

ISBNs: 9781009663250 (HB), 9781009289481 (PB), 9781009289504 (OC)
ISSNs: 2633-3309 (online), 2633-3295 (print)

Contents

1 Introduction: Emergence and World Englishes   1

2 The Theory of Complex Dynamic Systems   7

3 Turning Complex Dynamic Systems Theory into Linguistic Reality: The Central Role of Usage and Constructions   31

4 Complex Dynamic Systems Theory as Applied to World Englishes   35

5 Toward Agent-Based Modeling of Varieties Emergence Using NetLogo   65

6 Conclusion: World Englishes Keep Rolling   69

References   73

1 Introduction: Emergence and World Englishes

How different are World Englishes (WEs) from their metropolitan donor varieties and from each other, and why have these differences evolved and become firmly established? Indirectly, this question touches upon even broader, more fundamental ones: how are language varieties related to each other, and how does Language "work"? In the early phase of the discipline of WEs (and still in some branches of linguistics), languages and language varieties were conceptualized as discrete, separate entities. More recent thinking has tended to downplay discrete nation-based distinctions and to highlight mutual interactions, contact-induced changes, and linguistic forms as floating resources (Blommaert 2010; see Section 4.1). Extending this line of thinking significantly, in this Element, I am proposing a novel approach and explanation, arguing that languages and language varieties are best understood as perpetually fluctuating, highly complex interactions between a large number of agents and attributes, best to be accounted for by the scientific theory of Complex Dynamic Systems.

English is the world's leading language today by far – this is simply a trivial statement. In addition to being used as the default choice in transnational and "lingua franca" communication of whatever kind (in international politics, business, academia, tourism, etc.), it has come to be rooted as national, official, semi-official or practically most widely used language in about 100 countries all around the globe (for lists, see McArthur 1998, 2002; for a map, see Schneider 2020a:64). In these countries, stable varieties with distinct properties of their own (on the levels of phonology, lexis, grammar, and pragmatics) have emerged (such as Canadian, Singaporean, Indian, Nigerian, Ghanaian, or Australian English). The label "World Englishes" has been widely accepted as a summary designation of both these varieties and the scholarly discipline that intensely investigates their structural properties and sociopolitical settings. Most of these varieties are "Postcolonial Englishes" (see Schneider 2007), products of British (and rarely American) colonial expansion since the seventeenth century, including countries where the majority of speakers are native or first-language (L1) speakers of English, such as the United States or New Zealand, perceived as (modified) continuations of erstwhile British English (BrE). In many other former colonies, national varieties, which have often been called "New Englishes" (NEs), have evolved – second-language (L2) forms of English in multilingual contexts created by the process of colonial linguistic re-rooting under language contact conditions. In recent decades, however, globalization and the "transnational attraction" of English (Schneider 2014) have produced distinct forms (and usage contexts) of English also in countries with no British colonial background, such as Korea

(Rüdiger 2019), the Netherlands (Edwards 2016), or Namibia (Schröder 2021), producing, consequently, "Korean English," "Dutch English," "Namibian English,"[1] and others, respectively. In general, the distinction between postcolonial and nonpostcolonial varieties has been downplayed increasingly, and many similarities have been identified (Buschfeld & Kautzsch 2017, 2020). Since roughly the 1980s, the discipline of WEs, investigating and describing these varieties, has grown tremendously; access to it and survey representations can be found in many useful textbooks (Mesthrie & Bhatt 2008; Schneider 2020a), handbooks (Filppula, Klemola & Sharma 2017; Nelson, Proshina & Davis 2020; Schreier, Hundt & Schneider 2020), and other resources.

World Englishes are conventionally seen as distinct linguistic systems, separate from though related to their respective "parent/donor varieties." They are commonly regarded as "daughter varieties" of (mostly) British or (occasionally) American English (AmE), similar in some respects but distinct in others, with specific words, pronunciation habits, and grammatical patterns of their own, which are unique to certain regional or national varieties and contribute to constituting their independent systemic status. The assessment of these distinctive, innovative features is often a topic of quite some controversy, especially in local contexts where for historical and social reasons the erstwhile donor variety (typically BrE) is still considered to be the only "pure" and "correct" one, to be striven for in language teaching (see Schneider 2023). Consequently, when judging innovative structural properties of these varieties, utterances are commonly classified as "grammatical"/"acceptable" or not, or, in prescriptive and often educational contexts, "correct" or "wrong." There are many discussions in WEs and applied linguistics as to whether or when structurally unusual phenomena observed in NEs are errors or emerging properties, to be recognized as such (see Mukherjee & Hundt 2011).

This categorial line of thinking on different language varieties, viewing them as discrete and distinct entities[2] and their features as locally established and acceptable or not, is deeply engrained in linguistic thought and theorizing, and results from the dominant early phases and schools of linguistic theory development. In leading grammatical theories, languages are conventionally conceived of as discrete systems of interrelated rules or units and their mutual relations. To illustrate this and put it in context (even if this may be familiar to

---

[1] Obviously, such labels need to be problematized somewhat, since they posit an essentialist, entity-like understanding of varieties. For a discussion of the distinction between "X English" and "English in X," see Schneider (2007:50).

[2] Larsen-Freeman (2018b:82) labels this perspective "stasis – viewing it as a product, not a dynamic process." In contrast, she argues (and I fully agree) that "language is an inherently malleable, non-teleological system," and "learning a language is not about conformity to uniformity" (84).

many readers), let me take a short look at the theories that have dominated our understanding of "how language works" up until and through the twentieth century (and into the recent past), a short detour with a concise survey of established linguistic thinking, as it were.

Looking into and analyzing modern living languages began in early modernity (roughly the sixteenth and seventeenth centuries), when educated scholars in Europe came to apply the categories of ancient Greek and Latin, the only type of language analysis familiar to them, to living languages like English, thus establishing a line of thinking that came to be called "traditional grammar." It has fundamentally shaped traditions and concepts of language teaching in England, the western world, and elsewhere, and continues to be strongly influential to the present day. Educated language students will be familiar with many of its core concepts: Words are classified into "parts of speech" (word classes such as nouns, verbs, adjectives, etc.), and semantically interpreted grammatical categories (such as number, person, gender, or tense) are attached to these words, expressed by specific inflectional endings (e.g. *-s* for noun plurals, *-ed* for verbal past, *-er* for adjective comparatives, etc.). The modern thought that each language has a structure of its own that needs to be understood in its own right was unfamiliar to the proponents of these descriptions, who regarded Latin as the "ideal" language, sanctified by tradition. However, this scheme does not work well for modern English, a language that has changed from an erstwhile strongly synthetic type (with many inflectional endings in the Old English period) to a largely analytic language, with very few endings left and word class assignments being notoriously fuzzy and variable. Younger, internally important distinctive properties of modern English, which have evolved only in the last few centuries (such as aspect, word order, or the special role of an operator in the verb phrase; see Quirk et al. 1985) and which Latin does not have, were given short shrift and disregarded in school teaching. The attitude associated with this scheme, inherited from days of old, is thoroughly prescriptive – so unusual patterns (including innovative ones in NEs) are typically branded simply as "wrong" and "errors" to be avoided.

As is well known, modern linguistics as a scientific discipline started with structuralism, originated by Saussure (1916), and was then implemented in several regional schools in the first half of the twentieth century. In this framework, language is regarded as a purely synchronic system consisting of abstracted units of various kinds and levels (phonemes, morphemes, lexemes, etc.) that enter category relations through functional equivalence ("paradigmatic relations" of choice: *This animal is a dog/cat/horse/...*), delimit each other by contrast (*Willow is a cat.* [and hence not a dog/horse/...]), and build higher-order entities (like phrases or clauses) in chain-like syntagmatic relationships (*I love [my fluffy old cat]*). Language analysis operates mainly through inductively abstracting specific sequences of units categorized into paradigmatic classes. Hence, a sequence of symbols such as "Det + Adj + N" describes a prototypical noun phrase pattern (*my good friend, these lovely flowers,* ...). This type of structural approach is observation-based (as to how words behave, in which contexts and patterns they occur) and inductive (starting out from multiple empirical observations and then generalizing from them), and hence "objective," not based on preliminary dispositions. Thus, it is practically useful and has come to be influential, in particular methodologically (e.g. in corpus linguistics, where the behavior of words in context can be objectively observed and quantified). However, one obvious question is whether its purely surface-oriented, categorizing, and compositional approach is not somewhat reductive, whether it is sufficient for understanding how language works. Its rather mechanical procedure fails to recognize surface ambiguities, underlying relations and movements (such as corresponding active–passive structures), schematic structures, and the like.

Generative (transformational) grammar, originally the brainchild of Noam Chomsky, has become a strongly dominant discipline in linguistics, and since his first book in 1957 has gone through various developmental stages (such as Principles-and-Parameters, Move α, or Minimalism). Basically, it offers a highly abstract account of the human language faculty and is not primarily geared toward recognizing any language's distinctive traits. Its central goal is modeling "competence," the language knowledge of an "ideal speaker-listener, in a completely homogeneous speech community," a being that simply does not exist in reality. Actual linguistic behavior, "performance," is rejected as irrelevant (possibly containing errors and random deviations), and the approach is devoid of all interest in social and pragmatic contexts and variability (which has inspired the growth of sociolinguistics, pragmatics, and discourse analysis as more realistically grounded counter-tendencies since the 1960s). Essentially, generativism is a highly abstract rule-rewriting exercise – intellectually brilliant, perhaps, but with limited grounding in actual empirical observations of human behavior, constrained by axiomatic assumptions that deliberately exclude a huge amount of data, observations, and contextual conditions.

As to unexpected, "deviant" observations, structuralism would simply add further classification schemes to the existing set of possible patterns without evaluation, and in deductive generativism rules would have to be rewritten to account for ("generate") observed options. Both schools, however, and with them much of modern linguistics (with the exception of more recent theories as described in Section 3) build upon a notion of clear-cut entities, distinctions, and relations that deterministically describe what is possible or not in matters linguistic. Similarly to traditional grammar, clear-cut boundaries as to what exists and is possible in a language or not are assumed to exist.

Such deterministic and categorial thinking meets with its limitations quite often in communicative and attitudinal reality, however. "All grammars leak," as Sapir (1921:39) observed a century ago: All rules have exceptions, with or without a specific discourse function; grammars allow "multiple analyses" of the same surface structures and often show gradience in the assignment of forms to analytical categories (Quirk et al. 1985), and so on. Similarly for the relationship between varieties: They show similarities and differences, they overlap in some respects and with some forms but not in others (see Section 4 for an application to WEs). Prescriptive thinking that posits clear-cut rules and distinctions between "right" and "wrong" may be pedagogically helpful to some extent and certainly helps to uphold conservative social divisions in societies (between those with and those without access to higher education, where these rules and myths are perpetuated); but it does not conform to the realities of linguistic behavior: It has often been argued and shown that "usage guides" prescribe rules that are not widely observed in natural conversations. Adhering to simple rules may conform to a deeply human desire for clarity, conformity, and guidance in a challenging world, and result from cognitive principles favoring clear-cut categorizations and binary divisions, but, regrettably, that is not how in most spheres of life reality works. Language is not mathematics.[3] Language, and life, for that matter, are inherently fuzzy.

Similar trends toward the dissolution of once clearly established realities have marked developments in many other disciplines, including the sciences. Take physics as a case in point: Newton's beautifully deterministic equations seemed to have offered a solution to all puzzles regarding the revolution of planets in orbit and movements of objects in time and space, until Einstein's relativity came and overthrew it all. And that is not to talk of Heisenberg's indeterminacy principle or the insights of quantum physics. Nature and life are simply immensely complex processes. And it is time to recognize that this applies to language as well, and to ask which insights may result from this. Furthermore, the natural and social sciences do provide us with insights and theoretical frames that may also serve to advance our understanding of how languages, including WEs, "work."

Consequently, in this Element I advocate an alternative approach to theorizing on the nature of linguistic evolution, the emergence of language varieties, and I apply it specifically to the domain of WEs. I suggest that language and

---

[3] See Chambers (2003:26–38) for a similar criticism of the "categorial" approach from the perspective of modern variationist sociolinguistics.

language varieties should be integrated into and highlighted from the scientific sphere of Complex Dynamic Systems (CDSs). This is a scientific framework, a meta-theory, that has been growing strongly over the last few decades and that has been immensely successful in explaining many processes, properties, and relations in many natural and social sciences. Complex Dynamic Systems are systemic relations that, as the name suggests, are complex (i.e. consist of many locally interacting agents and components) and dynamic (i.e. continuously evolving in time and space – in addition to many other, more specific properties; see Section 2.2). They produce networks of higher-order interrelationships, and they are self-organizing, bringing about novel functional entities without a steering authority. I presuppose the basic assumption (standing behind this Element, and argued for by other linguists as shown in Section 2.3) that precisely these qualities characterize language and the relationship between language varieties as well, and that "Language," the human language faculty, and existing languages, constitute another important domain of life shaped by and manifesting CDS principles. Consequently, I argue that English(es), the sum total of all manifestations of this particular language, with no need for clear-cut boundaries, constitute a broad, important, multilayered domain (or fraction) within this CDS of Language, and that WEs, in turn, are components within such an overarching complex-systemic context.

In the next section, I introduce the approach and its theoretical framework, and, most importantly, I will discuss the properties that have been suggested as characteristic of CDSs. I believe it is necessary to introduce these principles and properties first, and independently, but I will provide cross-references to language whenever possible and offer sample applications to properties of English to build the connection from the outset. There have been earlier suggestions to apply this line of thinking to language studies, and I will briefly survey and discuss these (especially in Section 2.3). Many of the CDS principles, and some of these earlier language-related suggestions, are rather abstract in nature, and one core question is how these principles manifest themselves in linguistic evolution in everyday practice, on the ground, as it were. I believe that the school of usage-based linguistics, in association with construction grammar as a mode of formally modeling some of these interrelationships, offers a superb explanation of how emergence and evolution happen (see Hoffmann 2022:2.1), and so I will discuss these in some detail in Section 3. In Section 4, I will zoom in on the domain of WEs more specifically and will provide many illustrative examples showcasing select properties of WEs, which highlight how specific principles of CDSs manifest themselves in structural reality (with these principles as organizing guideline, similar to Section 2.2). And finally, in Section 5, I briefly illustrate how agent-based modeling, a procedure that is routinely employed to simulate and understand CDSs, can be applied to model the emergence of novel features of WEs, using the freeware programming environment NetLogo.

2 The Theory of Complex Dynamic Systems

2.1 Origins, Definitions, and Applications

Compared to other branches of the sciences, the theory of CDSs is relatively young: It can be traced back to precursor disciplines from the earlier twentieth century and to the work of some individual scholars, notably mathematicians, who laid foundations even earlier (see Larsen-Freeman 2017:12–13), but as a coherent framework it has evolved strongly and become influential in various subdisciplines of the sciences since roughly the 1960s (for a historical survey, see Mobus & Kalton 2015:32–40). It has been established and is growing vigorously in the natural and social sciences, with a wide range of successful applications in biology, medicine, social organization, natural phenomena, technology, businesses, and other disciplines. It captures basic properties of many domains in life marked by complex systemic relationships that are perpetually developing, with many agents and units that are interconnected, exchange information (in a very general sense) just locally, without any overarching steering authority, and thereby build something larger (so that the whole is more powerful than the sum total of its parts, a consequence of nonlinearity). The theory of CDSs argues against reductionism and categorial, deterministic thinking and highlights the productive power of interacting multi-agent systems without central control. It is a "holistic," "cross-disciplinary" approach, though at this stage not yet a fully-fledged theory with a "canonical" form but rather a "meta-science" (Mobus & Kalton 2015:3), a "transdisciplinary" "metatheory" (Larsen-Freeman 2017:14, 21).

Terminology is still somewhat unstable – the framework comes under varying labels such as systems science, complexity science, or theory of complex adaptive systems. The latter has been widely adopted when applied to language, but I prefer "CDS" because this term captures two of the most central properties of such systems (and "adapt" to me implies a given target [to what?], while here we witness a continuous process of different components evolving through time, influencing each other mutually).[4] By now the approach has been widely accepted and applied in the natural and social sciences, and established as a major all-encompassing research branch in itself, with powerful institutions devoted to developing it further (e.g. Max Planck Institutes for Dynamics and

---

[4] For a discussion of terminological issues with the same outcome, see de Bot (2017).

Self-Organization, for Intelligent Systems, or for the Dynamics of Complex Technical Systems). Its leading, longest-standing global research center is the Santa Fe Institute in New Mexico.[5] It offers a wide range of activities and resources (see complexityexplorer.org), including many courses on specific CDS-related topics (like Rand 2024 on agent-based modeling). The Institute promotes the CDS theory through several publications, for example Mitchell (2021; a recommendable, slightly technical introduction), or a lecture by its president on the epistemology of complexity science (Krakauer 2023). Other introductions and surveys that I have found useful include Bossomaier and Green (2000), Johnson (2009), Holland (2014), Mobus & Kalton (2015), and Jensen (2022). Researchers into CDSs have investigated the nature of developmental processes and outcomes in many domains of life, including ant colonies and many other life and ecology associations (e.g. tropical rainforests), the human brain (Bossomaier 2000), the economy (including markets), social networks (Buchanan 2003), or the growth of cities, to name but a few. The discipline's main tools are computational modeling and simulations (Mitchell 2021; Rand 2024; see Section 5).

Conceptual basics and processual explanations of CDS have their roots in nonlinear equations in mathematics described by chaos theory (e.g. Gleick 1987), one of its major precursor frameworks. Nonlinear equations have distinctive and apparently "strange" properties, such as extreme sensitivity to (minimal variation in) initial conditions, which may lead to qualitatively different leaps and outcomes, and the fact that after very many iterative, recursive runs of the equation the resulting phase model tends to approximate self-similar "attractor" states, something like order. Chaos theory is mostly seen as a core branch, one particular type, of CDSs (see, e.g., Guastello & Liebovitch 2009; Johnson 2009:ch. 3; Mitchell 2021:units 2.1, 2.6, 2.7). The core property of nonlinearity is usually taken to be shared (Mufwene et al. 2017:2; Larsen-Freeman 2018a:52) or even central to both disciplines: "Non-linear behaviour is one of the cornerstones of complexity" (Bossomaier & Green 2000:7; see also Mobus & Kalton 2015:202, 251–2, 592). Some central properties (e.g. the interrelationship of order and chaos, or bifurcation) derive from chaos theory.

Complex Dynamic Systems are characterized by a range of distinctive core properties, with the most important and relevant of them to be surveyed and contextualized in the next few sections. In each case CDS properties will be defined and described in their own right, but these descriptions will be followed by brief language-related observations or examples from English, to imply the claim (and hopefully make it compelling) that both are inherently related.

---

[5] www.santafe.edu/.

Section 4 will then be devoted to showcasing the application of these principles to WEs in greater breadth and detail.

2.2 Properties of Complex Dynamic Systems – and Effects in Language

While there is no generally accepted finite listing of the distinctive properties of CDSs in the discipline, and different authors define the notion slightly differently and highlight varying aspects, there is a basic consensus on some core components that constitute and characterize CDSs. I subdivide them into and present them as eight different central properties that encompass the most important qualities under discussion. In each case, I circumscribe the property in question as presented by CDS theorists before I consider some reflections and voices on its applicability to language in general and English in particular.

2.2.1 Systemness

In CDS theory, "a system is a whole of some sort made up of interacting or interdependent elements or components integrally related among themselves" (Mobus & Kalton 2015:73–74). This seems a rather trivial notion, but of course it constitutes a fundamental prerequisite for complexity to emerge. Systems are to be understood by knowing the units they are built of (and possibly relevant associated attributes) and the relations between them.

It is self-evident and axiomatic in linguistics that this holds for language as well, that languages are systems. The idea was introduced by Saussure (1916), the founding father of structuralism, who argued that language is a "system of signs" (and signs, in turn, are defined as pairings of *signifié* and *signifiant*, meaning and formal expression). Systemic relations mean that synchronically, at a given point in time and in a single language, units on several levels (phonemes, morphemes, lexemes) enter mutual relations of various kinds. Fundamentally, these relationships are either syntagmatic or paradigmatic. In syntagmatic ("chain"-type) relations items follow each other and jointly build a higher-order unit. For example, sounds build words (/m/+/æ/+/n/ > *man*), words build phrases (*the+old+man* is a prototypical noun phrase), and phrases build clauses ([*The old man*]$_{NP}$ [*is writing*]$_{VP}$ [*a letter*]$_{NP}$.). Paradigmatic ("choice"-type) relations hold virtually between units that can be exchanged for each other (can undergo "substitution" and stand in "contrast" to each other): they can fill the same slot, they function equivalently (and thus functionally defined constituent classes can be identified). For example, in the word *man*, the final consonant can be substituted by /t/, yielding another word, *mat*, and in the clause the object noun phrase slot after *writing* could also be filled by a single word (*something*) or a clause (*what he cannot tell*), showing the functional equivalence of these types of units. Evidently, any linguistic construction in any language builds on and exemplifies relationships of that kind. And the examples illustrate the important distinction and relation between function (what a unit does in context) and form (how it can be realized), similar to Saussure's sign concept and leading to the notion of constructions (see Section 3).

2.2.2 Complexity

This property, embedded in the name of CDS, is characterized by a very large number of independent agents or objects with specific attributes who keep interacting in manifold ways and exchanging information (including attributes) locally, but without a steering authority. In these interactions, which may be both collaborative and competitive, they may congregate to build larger, more complex entities and hierarchies to serve specific contextual needs and functions (e.g. cells build organs, and organs are core parts of a body). It is noteworthy, however, that being complex in the CDS sense is not the same as merely being "complicated," that is, consisting of many entities with relations that are difficult to understand.[6] The latter certainly constitutes a condition for the former, but complex systems are "quantitatively difficult to keep track of," involving "properties of many different independent components" (Jensen 2022:3). They are aggregates, characterized by the entire set of properties discussed here, most importantly emergentism and auto-organization. In other words, it is characteristic that new entities are being built, that the emerging whole is more powerful than the sum of its parts,[7] and cannot simply be deduced from knowing its components. In principle, however, complexity itself is a complex notion, a view of a world perched between order and disorder that is best looked at through the lens of a specific discipline applying it (Krakauer 2023).

The growth of complexity is of course closely related to the development of network relations and the emergence of new higher-order entities, possibly with new functions. Complex systems evolution therefore tends to increase diversity and functional specialization (Holland 2014:44–45).

The relevance of this principle to languages is equally self-evident and uncontroversial. As stated earlier, in languages, units combine to build larger sequences and constituents, steered by functional needs, and the resulting complex entities are often not transparent and information-richer than the set

---

[6] In the same vein, complexity theorists "make a distinction between restricted and general complexity" (Larsen-Freeman 2017:14).

[7] This idea, that "the collective of many interacting components can possess properties that are different and richer than those of the individual components" (Jensen 2022:12), can in fact be traced back to Aristotle (15).

of components. In this process, patterns and components of various kinds and magnitudes interact, both fundamentally in CDSs and in language as an application case. Consider Krakauer's (2023) statement: He illustrates "complexity science" as steering a compromise, at a certain level of organization, between constraints of construction, constraints of matter, and fit defined as the level of granularity of observations. To me this sounds very much like a description of language evolution, where (as many examples in this Element show) we observe interactions between language levels (e.g. phonological changes triggering morphosyntactic rearrangements), between constituents and constructions (e.g. changes of one sound pattern influencing articulatory conditions for another, words copying meanings, or constructions expanding their properties and range of applications), or between languages (in multilingual contact settings). All of these processes increase complexity.

Complexity in languages has been a fashionable topic of linguistics in recent years (see Miestamo et al. 2008; Sampson & Trudgill 2009; Kortmann & Szmrecsanyi 2012; Culicover 2013; Newmeyer & Preston 2014), though often this relates merely to different levels of being "complicated" as just defined. Tamaredo (2020:ch. 2) offers a useful and competent survey of these discussions, including the tendency to reject the erstwhile axiomatic assumption of all languages being equally complex, definitions of the notion based on the difficulty of acquisition and use (for speaker and hearer), the role of contact (generally assumed to cause simplification; see Schreier 2005), and attempts at measuring complexity quantitatively. Lund and colleagues (2022) repeatedly thematize the relationship between a wider, general and a more narrow, technical, CDS-inspired understanding of complexity.[8]

Complexity in language operates on two levels, the intralinguistic and extralinguistic ones.

Language-internal relations are conventionally understood as hierarchies of units that are mutually constitutive and that build higher-order functional units, as just shown. And this relation expands beyond sentence constituents to the level of utterances and discourse: clauses are constituents of utterances and sentences, which build discourse and texts. An additional, recursive level of complexity arises from the fact that some of these units can be mutually hierarchically constitutive: phrases are constituents of clauses, and clauses can be constituents of phrases. In line with CDS definitions of complexity, its

---

[8] Massip-Bonet and colleagues (2019) produced a collective volume which adopts a very wide understanding of complexity. A small number of contributions, notably Massip-Bonet (2019), who basically provides definitions of relevant and related terms, discuss aspects of CDS, but most others address various issues of human sciences, cognition, ecology, sociolinguistics, and discourse, with hardly any connections to the theory itself.

understanding in linguistics correlates with the number of units involved and the nature of their hierarchies. Strictly language-internal complexity also arises from ease of processing and acquisition including features like predictability and regularity. For instance, Tamaredo (2020) mentions "irregularities, new semantic/pragmatic distinctions into the grammar, or distinctions that are not transparently coded" (35) as characteristic features increasing complexity.

Language-externally, speakers can be viewed as agents in line with CDS conditions: there are large numbers of interactants, with different acquisition input histories and sociocultural backgrounds and consequently idiosyncratic idiolects, adopting varying identities and social roles and attributing different prestige assignments to their utterances. Clearly this offers room for all kinds of complexity to emerge. And the two levels also combine and interact in multiple ways: the usage of specific language forms co-varies with sociolinguistic parameters like class, gender, or style; speakers may select and enregister particular forms as increasingly indexical of social parameters; and the entire set of formal choices to encode a message and functional associations undergoes continuous variation and change – which leads us to the next CDS property.

2.2.3 Perpetual Dynamics

CDSs are always in flux, marked by continuously ongoing changes, adjustments, and modifications of system components in interaction and their relations over time, a perpetual process that has no starting point and never stops. In fact, in complexity science, it is not the agents, components, or "objects" that are viewed as central but the processes themselves; the world is "perceived as a nested hierarchy of processes" (Jensen 2022:13).[9] One interesting question is whether change proceeds fairly continuously or rather via "punctuated equilibria," with stretches of stability (periods of stasis) typically interrupted and altered by bursts of intense change (in line with the S-curve pattern in Figure 1; cf. Kretzschmar 2015:122–23).[10] "[T]he dynamics of complex systems commonly involve intermittent bursts of activity" (Jensen 2022:71).

There are some general principles and options of how systems may or tend to evolve (see Jensen 2022:ch. 3), but due to the large number of variables involved, the possibility of new players (e.g. through mutations) emerging

---

[9] For example, "Molecules are made up of quantum processes. The brain is made up of neuronal processes and the atmosphere is made up of electrochemical and thermodynamical processes." (Jensen 2022:13)

[10] The same pattern characterizes many evolutionary processes in life and other complex systems – think of the slow motions of the earth's tectonic plates suddenly interrupted by earthquakes, the periods of heightened financial crises in markets, and so on.

on the scene, and possible special effects of non-linear but also linear dependencies, forecasting future system states is practically impossible. Many systems tend to oscillate between forces strengthening order or disorder, respectively, and thus to return to near-equilibrium states. Typically, there are "lever points" (Holland 2014:25), where small directed actions cause substantially magnified effects (remaining within the same systemic arrangements) through aggregation. However, disruptive processes leading to different system states, often rather quickly, are also possible, for instance when some variable moves beyond a critical "tipping point" producing abrupt changes, or when exponential increase with feedback effects (a "more-begets-more" process) produces a distribution of a different magnitude. Also, neither effect sizes nor agent properties are stable, so, for instance, mutated properties may substantially affect the evolutionary directionality of a system or subsystem.

Again, this is equally self-evident and uncontroversial for languages and English(es). Language transmission from one generation to the next, also involving constant processes of change, is equally perpetually rolling. In fact, linguistic forms and habits are not even or mainly passed on across generations, but this transmission process happens all the time, irrespective of time scale: every single utterance always manifests and realizes the system, reiterates and reproduces linguistic usage; and every utterance is shaped by and at the same time influences and has the potential to modify future utterances produced by surrounding speakers (see Section 3).

Historical linguistics, the discipline studying the evolution of languages across different periods way back in time, tends to conceptualize select stages (such as Old English) as holistic, fairly stable units, but that is an idealization, too. In reality, transmission from caregivers to infant acquirers proceeded then as it does now, all the time and everywhere – there has been an unbroken chain of transmission, for example, from "Germanic" to "Old English" to "Middle English" to "Early Modern English" to "Modern English," without any interruption. Parameters and precise conditions varied at different points in time and space, of course, so depending on extralinguistic history more or fewer contact effects will have filtered in, but fundamentally the wheel of evolution and change has always been in motion, for each individual and, compositionally, in society at large.

This process of transmission comprises both elements of continuity, perpetuation across time without substantial modification, with sounds, words and patterns passed on and shared largely identically across periods and varieties, and discontinuity (i.e. change, innovation, and the adoption of elements from contact languages (with which speakers got in touch as a consequence of external conditions)). To illustrate continuity, practically all varieties of English have a sound /p/, a lexeme *hand*, and a NP pattern with a Det-Adj-N constituent sequence (*this interesting novel*). In addition, there is always a potential for continuous change, including internal innovation and modification as well as a possible impact of contact effects, bringing in novel forms and habits from other languages. There are numerous publications in linguistics both on principles of language change (e.g. Aitchison 2012; Chambers & Schilling 2013; Bybee 2015) and on processes and effects of language contact (e.g. Thomason 2001; Winford 2003; Matras 2020; Hickey 2020; Mufwene & Escobar 2022; Adamou & Matras 2023), and of course there is a myriad of individual studies and documentations of either. Obviously, external, contact-induced modifications are particularly important for investigations of WEs, which always originated in contexts of migration and multilingual interactions, but the elementary internal processes of change are potentially effective there as well, of course.

As an illustration of these principles (with the story to be continued later as to the evolution of WEs), let me briefly recapitulate the development of modal verbs in English(es), from the beginnings to some present-day branches (see Lightfoot 1979; Denison 1993:292–339; Fischer & van der Wurff 2006:146–52). As is well-known to language historians, in pre-Old English times some Proto-Indo-European perfect verb forms were semantically reinterpreted as (resultative) forms with present time meanings (the so-called "preterite-present verbs"). In Old English these verbs had full verb properties: they were main verbs, and some had direct objects, two properties which their German cognates have retained to the present day (e.g. *ich kann das*) but which English lost along the way (*I can that). Also, they had nonfinite forms, unlike today's English modals. In the transition from Middle English to Early Modern English these verbs were reanalyzed as auxiliaries (modal auxiliaries, more precisely), increasingly gaining the distinctive so-called "NICE" properties (being used in special ways for negation, inversion in interrogatives, "code" in elliptical structures, and emphasis); this can be seen as an instance of self-organizing emergence (see 2.2.6). Furthermore, they no longer allow direct objects and cannot be used without full verb predicates (cf. *I can do that*); they come to lack nonfinite forms (*to can, *caning); and their semantics has changed in distinctive ways, getting restricted to epistemic or deontic meanings (here we see network relations between different verb classes as to their structural behavior in effect). In present-day English many modals have been shown to be losing ground, to the point of being partly disappearing (e.g. in the cases of *may* for permission, *ought to*, or *shall*); conversely, new modals (*gonna*, *gotta*, *wanna*, ...) keep emerging, and the use of semi-modals (*be going to*, *have to*, ...) increases (Krug 2000; Leech et al. 2009:71–117). So, over more than

1,500 years usage conditions, associated attributes and relations between linguistic entities have continuously been changing, and the story continues.

Remarkably, there is a strong and explicit parallel in modelling the spread of innovations in society between CDS theory and linguistics: both have identified the "S-curve" as a typical representation of the diffusion dynamism, a model of the phase and state transitions that an innovation passes through. An S-curve (see Figure 1) is a sigmoid function, mathematically speaking, which has been shown to describe processes of spread in populations. The horizontal axis shows the progress of time, the vertical axis the intensity of the process in question, e.g. the spread of an innovation.

Figure 1 shows how new properties spread in a population over time, affecting an increasing proportion of a population. S-curves of diffusion show typical phases: a slow start, then a quick rise through the population, and finally a slow trailing off (typically leaving some residuals unaffected by the innovation, a cause of irregularity). This has been observed to be a common type of process in many domains. For CDS, Mobus & Kalton (2015) state: "The S-shape of the logistic function is generated when processes are characterized first by an exponential rise followed by an exponential deceleration to level off at a maximum" (215; see their graph 6.1, which applies the scheme to population biology). Interestingly, the growth of the number of connections in a network, sometimes called the "connectivity avalanche," follows the same pattern (Seeley 2000:64), and this applies to the diffusion of innovations in a society in general (Rand 2024: section 4).

In sociolinguistics, the S-curve is also the generally accepted model for how linguistic innovations spread in social space, in a characteristic "slow-quick-quick-slow" pattern (Kroch 1989; Labov 1994:65–67). A classic application to the history of English is the work by Ellegård (1953), who plotted the spread of

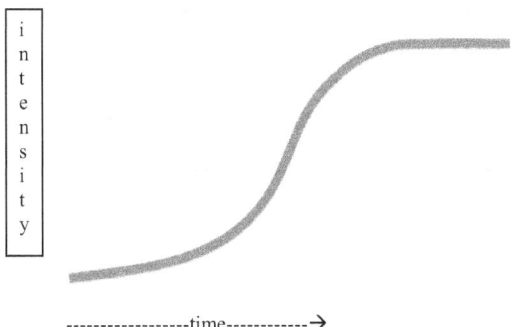

Figure 1 The S-curve as a diffusion model (produced by Alan Taylor 2013, Wikimedia Creative Commons 3.0 license)

different innovative functions of the verb *do* between 1400 and 1700 and also found a rather straightforward S-curve. Change is thus understood as incremental, not discontinuous – but non-linear! A meta-study by Nevalainen (2015) puts the model to the test and finds it largely confirmed and basically descriptively adequate for the vast majority of longitudinal changes investigated. Hence, both in biological CDSs and in language innovations diffuse in identical ways, in a S-curve shape. The fact that both are obviously related, being driven by the same evolutionary principle, can be seen as an important piece of support for the claim that language is also a CDS.

2.2.4 Network Relationships

In CDS theory, "systems are … networks of relations," "the components are connected in various relations" (Mobus & Kalton 2015:137), often indirectly, in a chain-like fashion.[11] Multiple agents are involved and connected with each other as in a network, but there is no overarching steering authority; all changes happen as consequences of small-scale local interactions, with agents adhering to the same or similar rules. Interactions involve the exchange of information (and possibly as a consequence adjustments of an agent's attributes). Typically, agents interact only with their immediate neighbors, and have no access to information on the system as a whole or on attributes of distant agents. Still, after many iterative runs of local information exchanges governed by certain rules of mutual interaction and influence, larger-scale systematic patterns may emerge: iterations give way to complexity (Mitchell 2021, units 2.2–2.4 and 5). Examples of real-life networks vary widely in character, comprising, for example, neurons, airline routes, the internet, the power grid, banks, etc. (Mitchell 2021, 9.1) Most real-life networks are "small-world" networks, with few links required to any other member via long-distance links and hubs (Mitchell 2021, 9.3; Buchanan 2003).

Networks depend on links between the individual agents, and typically in collective systems links are associated with shared properties which are unequal in weight and importance. For understanding the evolution of a network it is therefore important to identify the nodes and assess their relative strength and character. Typically, networks then can be broken down to sub-systems on several levels, based on subsets of commonalities, which participate in the interaction dynamics.

The growth of networks proceeds through several phase changes, often in S-curve-like massive connectivity increases, and it is thus closely related to the notions of emergence and self-organization, criticality (since in some states

---

[11] Network science, closely related to mathematical graph theory, is, in fact, generally considered a distinct, though closely related, paradigm (see Buchanan 2003).

adding further nodes may tip the balance and cause the system to change states), and transitions between stability and chaos (Seeley 2000). Structures emerge through the incremental build-up of nodes in digraphs, and possibly circuits, and ultimately more complex configurations. Seeley (2000) provides a complex survey of network dynamics and types, marked by different kinds of links and nodes and leading to self-organization and emergence.

Evidently, languages also operate in network relations between many different entities, marked by "complete interconnectedness" (de Bot et al. 2007:8). As stated before (in Section 2.2.2), this applies and can be viewed from two perspectives, extra- and intra-linguistically: networks between many individuals as speakers, and network interrelationships between linguistic forms and functions.

Language is always communication between speakers, and normally there are many of them, for example in a speech community. And they constitute a social network, obviously: The language-external perspective recognizes the fact that the development of linguistic forms depends upon social relationships and interactions between speakers as agents in a CDS of language. Thomason & Kaufman (1988), for instance, explicitly stated that "the history of a language is a function of the history of its speakers" (4). And usage-based thinking, advocated here (see Section 3), sets language production by speakers in interaction, and that means network relations, at its center.

In a language-internal perspective, network-like interrelationships exist between linguistic items, i.e. forms and constituents, constructions, and language levels (see Hoffmann 2022:9 for an example of a network of ditransitive constructions). Both syntagmatic and paradigmatic relations are cases in point, involving many linguistic units of various kinds to either build something larger together or to fill an information slot; network relations hold between entities both in a chain relationship of compositionality and in a choice relationship of mutual exclusion. For example, in *John built a hut* the word *hut* stands in a network relation both with *John*, *build* and *a* (with which it builds a clause) and, by implication, with words like *palace*, *condo* or *cupboard* (which John could have built but, we are told indirectly, hasn't).

Such network-like intralinguistic systemic relations may hold between individual entities but also between composites of entities and more abstract composites, levels, and attributes, for example across levels of language organization (like phonology, morphology, lexis, or grammar). As a nice example of this, let us have a brief look at the loss of endings in the history of English, and consequently the change of the character of English from a largely synthetic language (with many inflectional endings) to a largely analytic one (with very few suffixes left), a most fundamental transition.

Indo-European, Germanic and Old English were strongly synthetic languages, rich in grammatical suffixes.[12] The change started inconspicuously, with the "Germanic Main Stress Rule," which fixed stress on first syllables of words in pre-Old English times. Stressed initial syllables cause a weakening of the phonation stream in later, especially final syllables, which, in turn, produces the weakening of full vowel qualities (to schwa, or, later, nothing) in final syllables. In Old English, this reductive tendency was amplified (presumably) by intensive contact with the Scandinavians' Old Norse, supporting simplification, here the loss of endings. So gradually, most inflectional endings disappeared (and lack of marking of course also decreases the amount of order in the sub-system). For example, Old English *sunu*, with a full final vowel, became weakened Middle English *sune* and ultimately uninflected modern English *son*. However, the endings had had grammatical functions, expressing intrasentential relations (of identifying the subject or object in a clause, for instance), so their job needed to be done in some other way, compensated for by new grammatical means of expressing syntactic functions. Consequently, English developed a fixed Subject-Verb-Object word order and the strengthening of function words (a process of auto-organizing emergence, if we so wish). A former accusative ending became replaced by the direct object position immediately after the verb; the dative ending gave way to the preposition *to* plus the noun; the verbal subjunctive was weakened substantially, its function being taken over by modal verbs and modal adverbs, and so on. So the radical change of the character of English, unique among the Germanic languages, was motivated by a series of interacting causes and step-by-step influences, leading from stress to phonology to morphology and to syntax. Clearly these sequences and connections constitute a network, between individual linguistic forms and, more abstractly, systemic patterns (manifested by forms).

2.2.5 The Interplay of Order and Chaos

Chaotic systems, "whose behavior appears to follow a regular pattern but not entirely" (Mobus & Kalton 2015:202), marked by reiterations of nonlinear equations and thus ultimately unpredictable feedback loops (251–52), constitute one major form of CDS. In chaotic systems many state variables are coupled, typically (though not obligatorily) non-linearly, sometimes adaptively (so that the conditions of connectedness change, with strategies and principles of evolution modified

---

[12] Needless to say, as in other sample cases in this Element, I focus on relevant essentials; the story I am outlining here abstracts from details and is somewhat straightened and simplified, but the basic argument and evolutionary line is robust and uncontroversial.

during the process due to internally selective factors). But their behavior is not completely random (though unpredictable) – after a large number of iterative re-runs they tend to approximate or reach "attractor" states (see Section 2.2.8), where the system returns to self-similar periodic behavior for a while.

Such systems are characterized by the co-existence of order and chaos (in different sub-systems and at different times): there are "pockets of order" inside "chaos" (Gleick 1987), "a complicated mix of ordered and disordered behavior" (Johnson 2009:15), with order arising "in both time and space" (21). This is a consequence of the fact that especially in the worlds of nature and culture noise and regularity compete (Krakauer 2023). Broadly, relatively orderly sub-systems and relations can be understood as having comparatively few interactants with rather clear functional assignments, while chaotic sub-systems consist of large numbers of interactants with random, non-functional behavior. Transition from order and/or simplicity to chaos and/or complexity proceeds via phases of "turbulence" possibly producing "phase transitions"; CDSs tend to oscillate between both states. Nature exploits chaotic structures in such processes as "an important source of novelty and variety in living systems" (Green 2000:45).

While such pockets of order may (and tend to) occur unpredictably, they are not here to stay – "there is a natural tendency for something that is ordered to become disordered as time goes by" (Johnson 2009:25) – but not the other way around. This fact is ultimately caused by a very fundamental law of nature, the second law of thermodynamics, which states that in a closed system entropy (commonly taken to be a measure of disorderliness) always increases, and this process cannot be reversed. In other words, earlier orderly states will never return, but new ones are likely to arise somewhere. A central force generating increased order is feedback within system components, typically involving memory (which is "a form of feedback," Johnson 2009:67) of earlier interaction effects and possibly boosting it via circular feedback loops (cf. my earlier remarks on S-curve diffusion and the avalanche of network interconnectivity).

Obviously, this applies to languages and Englishes as well: At any point in time in a given variety, there are sub-systems which are relatively orderly (i.e. consist of a relatively small number of units with clear functional assignments and clear mutual delimitation) and sub-systems which are relatively disorderly (marked by a large number of units, irregularity, fuzziness, and functional overlaps).[13] And

---

[13] The dividing line between the two is intuitively straightforward but also a matter of more or less, not a categorial distinction. Rules in language tend to have exceptions, and changes affect many items of a certain type but usually leave some residual forms unaffected. Consequently, there is a thin transition line between complicated (sub)systems (with many entities the distribution of which is rule-governed and predictable) and complex or chaotic ones (where rules are no longer reliable predictors).

this is constantly subject to change: ordered subsystems may be disrupted and break down, but conversely systematicity may emerge in formerly chaotic subsystems.[14] An example of the first type of change is provided in the next paragraph; in general, it is assumed that rule-governed sound changes, especially if different laws of change interact and compete, may lead to less coherent, more disorderly sets of forms. The mechanism that materializes the second tendency is an increase of conventionalized associations between meaning (function) and form (pattern) in usage, clearly a manifestation of an increase of network relations and order based on feedback and memory as posited in CDS theory.

An example from the history of English, extending back across millennia, is the dissolution of the English strong verb system. For Indo-European, the conventional, generally accepted reconstruction, disregarding variability, posits a perfectly regular and predictable system, with verbs having four functionally distributed principal forms which had different degrees of stress assignment and, correspondingly, vowel variants. By Old English, internal effects caused disequilibria, and the system moved toward turbulence: Various interfering conditioned sound changes, triggered by different following sound environments, produced a rather complex but still somewhat predictable set of strong verb classes and forms, with different modified stem vowels. In the transition to Middle English (ME) the reduction of four principal verb forms to three caused the breakdown of whatever order may have been left. Variability as to which forms survived produced the rather chaotic set of several hundred unpredictable and idiosyncratic irregular verb forms which we find in English today. Even more turbulence, irregularity and chaos[15] characterize regional and social dialects, where forms such as *bring – brung, fight – fit, sit – sot, fetch – fotch, catch – cotch, take – tuck/tooken*, and others appear (Schneider 1989:90–114). On the other hand, English(es) have also developed counter-tendencies toward regaining order. One is regularization (since the establishment of "weak verbs" with dental suffixes for past in Germanic), adopting the cognitive principles of regularity, compositionality, and isomorphism, a consistent association of form (dental suffix *–ed*) and meaning ('past'). Some verbs became re-classified accordingly (e.g., Old English *helpan–healp–hulpon–holpen* became Modern English *help-helped-helped*), and again, even more so in dialects (where we find forms like *knowed, growed, gived*, etc.). Secondly, some new regularities of past tense formation have emerged. For example, Cheshire (1994) showed how the "ideaphone" /ʌ/, originally found in past tense forms like *flung, wrung*, or *stung*,

---

[14] One reviewer raises the interesting question whether there are any subsystems which are more immune (or, conversely, susceptible) to turbulence or disruption than others.

[15] Admittedly, the notion of "chaos" is used in a rather non-technical, metaphorical sense here, meaning something like "disorderly, unstructured, close to anything goes."

became more widely associated with the notion of 'past-ness', contributing to the formation of further, especially dialectal past tense forms such as *run, struck, wrung, done, sunk, drug, tuck*, or *brung* (see Schneider 1989:90–114), and, for example, to the ongoing massive spread of *snuck* for *sneaked* in Canada documented by Chambers (2006–07).

A notable subtype of chaotic behavior which is also obviously shared by CDSs and language is bifurcation. This term describes the fact that a single category splits into two.[16] It represents one of possible forms of behavior in chaotic systems described in "catastrophe theory" developed by the mathematician René Thom as a branch of chaos theory (cf. Guastello & Liebovitch 2009:12–15). Bifurcations are a simple ("first-order") type of "catastrophy," a functional discontinuity and sudden qualitative change at a specific, mathematically derived point, a transition point into chaos where a system may or may not change direction and may suddenly split into two co-existent states.

Obviously, this principle manifests itself in languages and Englishes as well, e.g. in historically documented instances of a single unit splitting into two, which is possible on several levels. An example from English phonology is the fact that Old English had a single high back short vowel /u/, which, however, in the course of time and in different sound environments split into today's /ʊ/ (as in *put, pull, butcher*, ...) versus /ʌ/ (in *but, pulp, butter, cut*, ...). Splits have also occurred in lexis, with one word acquiring two different shapes and meanings – so *flower/flour, urban/urbane, metal/mettle, shade/shadow, skirt/shirt, catch/chase*, and other pairs go back to originally the same cognate.

2.2.6 Emergentism and Self-Organization

Emergentism and "auto-organization," often termed "twin processes," are core properties of CDSs (related to network building) and central components of evolution in general: smaller, less complicated entities interact, form new linkages, and jointly build gradually more complex functional units. This can be seen as a manifestation of the importance of a co-operative, complexity-building principle in life which can be taken to counter an emphasis on competition (e.g. the "survival of the fittest") and fragmentation (as in structuralism) as basic organizing forces. Such new complex, multi-unit organizational entities adapt mutually and with their environment to fulfill specific functions, producing higher-order, more complex sub-systems and functional organization levels – so the system overall is self-organizing toward creative emergence.[17] A "spiraling

---

[16] The mathematical basis of such splitting processes is spelled out in Jensen (2022:ch. 5).

[17] See Jensen (2022:section 1.2) for a survey of the growth of and scientific views on the notion of emergence and Jensen (2022:ch. 2) for types and properties of emergence. He defines the concept

cycle of increasing complexity," forming structures and possibly leading to order (from chaos), has been observed. Mobus & Kalton (2015:459–61, 476) describe it as follows: "systems can self-organize (i.e. become more complex) ... evolution is understood as a systematically produced trajectory of increasing complexity that need not be teleologically headed anywhere." Typically, emergence proceeds via steps of gradual synchronization of properties, a kind of diffusion process. For example, the brain requires synchronization of neurons (cf. Minelli 2009), and the financial market builds on uniform herding behavior of traders (cf. Jensen 2022:28–33), "individual oscillatory motion becoming coordinated across many components" (59). As a rather transparent example, consider the growth and development of big cities. Typically, they start out as a small group of settlers staying at a place to exploit its advantages (strategic location, fertile soil, natural resources, etc.). Success begets more success: It keeps growing, attracting more people, requiring the construction of roads, more powerful housing units, and congregation places, the development of specialized professions, the need for an administration, a security force, an educational system, health services, and so on, with each of these sub-systems complexifying and auto-organizing effective rules of their own and the sub-systems interacting with each other.

Importantly, emergence operates on specific levels (Krakauer 2023), within a certain range of operational parameters, "functionally closed protectorates" where the necessary and sufficient parameters to understand a system's future states, encoding some degree of entailment, are available. For example, to understand an AI system playing the game of Go it is sufficient to consider the board, moves and strategies, and there is no need to look at software code or hardware components. Similarly, understanding the mind does not require exact knowledge of the physiology of the brain. Emergence operates internally, and in some cases may be seen as something like a "black box" from the outside. Krakauer's discussion of CDS ontology implies that linguistic systems and sub-systems can be investigated and understood as emergent CDSs without needing to recur to bodily states, sound properties or the quantum-physical composition of speakers. Emergence results from interaction, not substance: "certain aspects of the emergent collective behaviour depend on so-called many-body effects, namely the cooperative collaborative effects generated by the interactions *between* the components and to a much lesser degree on the internal properties of the components" (Jensen 2022:22).

The diffusion of evolutionary novelty typically proceeds via "symmetry breaking" (Jensen 2022:section 2.5): Individual agents adopt properties against

---

as "the occurrence of properties or phenomena at the aggregate level, which the individual parts do not possess" (18).

the probabilities defined by the collective of agents, and such a "mutant offspring" (33) may then attract others and spread, thus introducing a sub-system with different properties. "Emergence of structure associated with the breaking of symmetry is a fundamental phenomenon which is seen as underlying the emergence of structure in hugely different situations" (34). In theories of language change this appears to correspond to Croft's (2000) distinction between "altered replication" (or innovation, when a linguistic entity is being modified in specific reproduction instances) and "propagation" (or diffusion, when a new linguistic form becomes preferred over others, i.e. spreads in the community).

In these processes, adaption, evolution and emergence go hand in hand, highlighting different aspects of largely the same or similar processes. Jensen (2022) states: "Adaptive evolutionary dynamics can be viewed as both an example of emergence and a very effective motor for generating emergent collective structure" (39), referring to evolution through Darwinian natural selection as a classic example (60–64). Characteristic processes include the emergence of a characteristic scale (at which an innovation most readily manifests itself), robust collective parameters, symmetry breaking (as just defined), the growth of networks, and intermittent dynamics, e.g. via a punctuated equilibrium (39). Adaptation is seen as a co-evolutionary selective pressure which gives direction to random mutations and variation by increasing the formation of similar types (e.g. species). Compared to evolutionary biology, in social dynamics natural selection through adaptation operates not through genome changes but through the reproduction of (modified) properties in interdependent agents, who modify their strategies based on experience (Holland 2014:6). This includes cultural evolution – the growth, decline and innovation of "the popularity of an idea and the invention of new concepts and ideas" (Jensen 2022:61). All of these aspects, obviously, apply to the evolution of a language variety as well, when an innovation originates and gets preferred in a community for some reason (perhaps because it is more transparent or simpler in its encoding of a meaning intended). The reproduction rate depends on interaction density with other agents and the fitness of mutations in context, which determine whether properties of co-evolving agents will multiply, mutate further, or die out.[18]

Again, this principle is evidently applicable to English(es) and languages as well. Larsen-Freeman (2013) states: "As new forms emerge through adaptation

---

[18] The "Tangles Nature" framework extensively discussed by Jensen (2022:68–69, 80–82 and 337–49), describing "co-evolving interacting agents giving rise to intermittent collective adaptive non-stationary dynamics" (349), seems particularly appropriate as an explanatory framework in the present context.

and co-adaptation, they self-organize into coherent patterns" (104). Beckner and colleagues (2009) put it pointedly: "Linguistic patterns are not preordained by God, genes, school curriculum, or other human policy. Instead, they are emergent" (18). Early work along these lines is a paper by Hopper (1987), who sees grammar as emergent (discussing essentially what has come to be called "grammaticalization").

A basic manifestation of this property in languages is simply the principle of compositionality[19]: small units jointly build larger constituents with a different function. This is illustrated by any higher-level construction (words built from sounds, phrases from words, clauses from phrases, etc.), e.g. in the build-up of complex lexemes (like *washing machine*, *unhappiness*, ...), idioms (e.g. *spill the beans*, *kick the bucket*), complex prepositions (*in spite of*; cf. Bybee 2010), and chunking and phraseologisms (i.e. constructions like *To tell you the truth; What is more; After all*; ...). And the principle then remains effective and further expands to more abstract compositional patterns. In Construction Grammar, for example, a progress from rather simple and concrete form-meaning pairings (words) toward the growth of increasingly abstract schematic constructions is posited (Hoffmann & Trousdale 2013). Examples of such schematic constructions include the indirect object constructions with the schema $SVO_{indir}O_{dir}$ (e.g. *he gave me a book*) or the comparative correlative construction *the Xer, the Xer* (e.g. *the older, the merrier*) (Hoffmann 2019). In fact, Hoffmann (2021) showed that developmentally more advanced World Englishes varieties show increased productivity in realizing schematic constructions, clearly a process of construction emergence. Grammaticalization, when formerly independent units come to co-occur regularly and ultimately fuse into single, complex units (with additional semantic and syntactic properties associated) also constitute one fairly clear manifestation of emergence in languages (cf. Beckner et al. 2009: 6–7; Kretzschmar 2015: 109–12). Chernyshova et al (2022) argue that recurrent, increasingly conventionalized patterns and multimodal practices in conversational interactions can be viewed as emergent complex and collaborative routines.

Two wider, related concepts in linguistics are worth mentioning in particular as early and indirect manifestations of the observation of such self-organizing tendencies in languages. In a classic book on *Language* Edward Sapir (1921: ch. 7) introduced the notion of "drift" in languages, an inbuilt trajectory of

---

[19] One reviewer points out that, going back to the philosopher Gottlob Frege, there is a finely graded distinction between compositionality, reflecting syntactic relations, constituency (being built from units with different functions), and contextuality (the impact of context for the interpretation of combined forms). These largely philosophical details do not play a role here; all these patterns and relations reflect emergentism and network relations.

"unconscious" long-term change toward more consistent typological properties (e.g. the loss of endings in English, a process rolling consistently for more than a thousand years by now). Keller (1994) posited the operation of an "invisible hand" in language change, an unintended directionality of evolutionary processes of linguistic change toward more consistent systemic relationships as the product of collective human agency, without any steering authority.[20]

2.2.7 Nonlinearity and Fractals

Chaos and complexity theory originally derive from the investigation of the properties of nonlinear equations in mathematics. Ideally, relationships between components and agents can be captured by non-linear functions, typically with feedback loops (so that the output of an activity / run becomes the input to a later re-run of the same function). Consequently, changes can spread very quickly and exponentially, and can also produce qualitative leaps. In reality, though, real-life systems (like the fairly well-known predator-prey cycle) have been shown to approximate nonlinear systems, but applications have often applied these concepts somewhat metaphorically (since often too many factors to be controlled for may have an impact), leaving strictly mathematical modelling to idealized simulation systems.[21]

A characteristic property of chaotic systems, resulting from nonlinear equations, is what is technically known as "sensitivity to initial conditions" and has come to be popularly widely known as "butterfly effect" (illustrated as the flapping of the wings of a butterfly causing a tornado some time later at a totally different place). Hence, a minimally slight difference of initial states leads to unpredictably large divergence of a system (or rather, two variants of a system) down the road: amplification in feedback loops may lead to a far-reaching qualitative leap.[22] This has important consequences for the time flow of such systems: as a matter of principle their evolution is explainable from hindsight but unpredictable in advance. Several phenomena commonly associated with CDSs ultimately derive from nonlinearity. Guastello and Liebovitch (2009) list "attractors, bifurcations, chaos, fractals, self-organization, and catastrophes" (36) as an inventory of new concepts which can be modeled as nonlinear functions offering entirely new ways of understanding change.

---

[20] However, as one reviewer pointed out, this theory has also been discussed critically, since it tends to downplay speaker agency as against some mysterious teleological target.

[21] In the same vein, Jensen (2022) states that while mathematics is at the basis of complexity science, "its conceptual basis can to a large extent be presented without mathematical formalism" (3) – which is what I am attempting to do here.

[22] This is difficult to model or understand, though, not only when applied to language but in general: "The complexities introduced by loops have so far resisted most attempts at analysis" (Holland 2014:39).

Consequently, as applied to a language as a CDS, the history and development of English (or any language) can be explained but not predicted, because small-scale distinctions (possibly via affecting other levels of organization) may have far-reaching, qualitative effects. A very strong example of such a process in the history of English, the loss of endings and its causes and steps, was showcased earlier in Section 2.2.4 on network relations: a small-scale phonotactic change (the fixing of stress) almost 2,000 years ago has ultimately led to the fundamental transformation of the typological character of English, from synthetic to analytic. Elsewhere (in Schneider 2020b) I spelled out details of what can be seen as another example of a butterfly effect, the long-time consequences of West Germanic "replacive lengthening" in English versus German, where a minimally widened variant condition of the sound environment in Anglo-Frisian for words to be affected by a sound change at that period (some 1600 years ago) produced a consistent phonotactic difference in lexical shapes between cognates in English (where nasals got lost in words such as *five* and *us*) but not German (compare *fünf, uns*).

An additional core property of chaotic systems, resulting from nonlinearity and iteration, is the fact that they are typically fractal, i.e. self-similar independent of scale: Patterns and relationships between components are self-similar irrespective of the magnitude of the observational level, whether microscopic or pertaining to the universe. Fractals do not follow a normal, Gaussian distribution (with some small, many average and some big objects) but break down to smaller and smaller similar patterns (trees to branches to twigs, for instance). A classic example, widely reproduced, is the Mandelbrot set (pictured in Figure 2, with colored surroundings), named after the concept's inventor: This

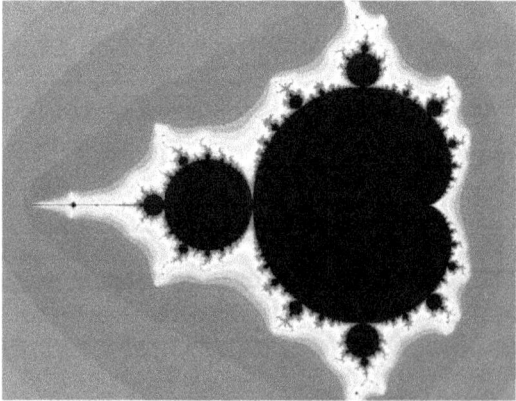

Figure 2 The Mandelbrot set (CC BY-SA 3.0, https://commons.wikimedia.org/w/index.php?curid=16063)

is a two-dimensional set produced by a mathematical formula where the visualization is always the same, no matter how deeply one zooms in in recursive magnifications. In nature, many phenomena have been shown to follow the same behavior (coastlines, snowflakes, leaves of ferns, river systems, blood vessels), though there the self-similarity operates only on a limited number of scales – they are "fractal-like" (Mitchell 2021: unit 3.2; cf. Jensen 2022: section 2.1 on systems with characteristic scales), or statistically but not geometrically self-similar (Guastello & Liebovitch 2009:17).

Fractals are characterized by dimensions which are, unlike the standard dimensions in space, not integers, i.e. they are not one-dimensional lines or two-dimensional planes but have a dimension between 1 and 2, and this dimensionality is a measurement of a fractal's density compression. In nature, fractals are an extremely efficient way of squeezing in an enormous amount of material (say, veins, or brain parts) into a small amount of space, with densely packed curves packed into higher-level self-similar curve lines (Mitchell 2021: units 3.3 and 3.4). Scaling theory implies that there are optimal levels of compression (Krakauer 2023), where "effective coarse-graining" ontologically offers a reasonable compromise between noise and order, losing some but not too many parameters, thus optimizing principles in local environments. A related, helpful concept is that of being "nested," every (sub-)system being part of another system (de Bot et al. 2007:8).

Fractals in language are not as directly visible as other CDS properties, but they appear to be identifiable and are possibly caused by communicative efficiency needs, a balance between saving cognitive and articulatory energy and sufficiently rich information encoding. A case in point is Zipf's law, a "power law" stating that the frequency of occurrence of a word in a corpus is inversely proportional to its rank in a frequency listing (Larsen-Freeman & Cameron 2008:109–111; Kretzschmar 2015:83–86). Hence, according to a "principle of least effort" this strikes a balance between hearer (who wants maximally efficient decoding, thus preferring familiar forms) and speaker (who needs a choice between simple and efficient encoding or the encoding of special, less predictable information) needs.

It is noteworthy that not all properties of CDSs are scale-free; in fact, exponential functions may produce and emergent systems may be marked by characteristic scales (Jensen 2022:23–26, 50–54).

2.2.8 Attractors

After a large number of recurrent iterative runs (time units) dynamic systems tend to approximate specific types of "attractors," subsets of their phase space –

relational shapes which are strongly self-similar but never fully identical (mathematically a consequence of nonlinear equations). Chaos theory distinguishes fixed-point, periodic, and chaotic (or "strange"), fractal attractors – self-similar space states which can be perceived as relatively orderly, so this property interacts with the interplay between order and chaos referred to earlier, and it is intrinsically connected with the notions of dynamics, change, and emergence: A "system diverges from its initial state and after a transient period settles into some attractor state," which may be "a simple equilibrium" or "a strange attractor" (Green 2000:26).

While the notion of attractors is rather precisely defined in chaos theory, its metaphorical application in other fields is often handled more loosely, indirectly building upon the meaning "something that attracts" in a wider sense. Cooper (1999) proposes the notion as relevant to language acquisition and change, with applications (involving the Northern Cities Shift in US dialects) strongly leaning toward mathematical, computational and information-theoretic procedures and viewing attractor patterns as competing with each other in a sociodynamic perspective. Larsen-Freeman and Cameron (2008) define attractors as "a region of a system's state space into which the system tends to move" (50), and apply it culturally to concepts as diverse as the gaits of a horse-and-rider system (trotting, galloping, etc.), British A-level examinations (resisting change as generally accepted behavior), explanatory notions (such as the knowledge that the earth rotates around the sun) or artefacts (e.g. a violin; 50–55). In a second-language acquisition context they also view "preferred paths within individual performances," counter-acting intra-individual variability, as "attractors" (153), and identify specific discourse patterns or fossilized states as attractors (180–185, 214; cf. de Bot et al. 2007:10, 15). This seems open to discussion: When the concept is applied to any kind of pattern or convention it is in danger of losing its conciseness and explanatory power.

Thus, the character and role of the attractor concept in languages calls for further consideration. Very basic conceptual relations between systemic choices may be regarded as fixed schemes which serve as attractors – for example, contrast as an elementary type of paradigmatic relation (for example, voice in English is either active or passive; and in the case of mediopassives form is pulled to the active but meaning to the passive frame). Individual linguistic items and structures that speakers aim at and produce in the process of information encoding may be seen as attractors. More generally, this may be taken to be closely related to the wider concept of "constructions" as in Construction Grammar (Hoffmann & Trousdale 2013; Hoffmann 2022; Laporte 2021; Ungerer & Hartmann 2023): the conceptual schemas in construction grammar (illustrated in Section 2.2.6, for example) clearly "attract" further lexical material to be used in the very same way (cf. Hoffmann 2014, 2021). Attractors in language can thus be also understood, fully in line with CDS thinking, as emergent patterns, "a probabilistic profile ... out of the state space of possible outcomes" (Kretzschmar 2015:137) in a dynamic evolutionary process. And they can drive language change, for example when a system "transitions from the basin of attraction of one attractor to the basin of another" (Cooper 1999:137).

2.3 Earlier Thinking on Language as a Complex Dynamic System

The idea that language, and any particular language, for that matter, constitutes a CDS is definitely not new – it has been around for the last two or three decades, and it is gaining ground, judging from the number of publications which address it or hint at it. However, at this point it is clearly still a marginal theoretical option, far from mainstream thinking. Interestingly, almost all such views have been voiced by linguists. In the literature on CDS, many application domains are discussed, but hardly ever language. Holland (2014) mentions language as a complex system, but does so rather incidentally,[23] and Krakauer (2023) refers to "biological linguistics and anthropology," which, however, he believes to be not quantitative.

In linguistics, some early, general suggestions considering the applicability of CDS thinking to language include Lindblom and colleagues (1984) on self-organization, Hopper (1987) on grammar as emergent, and Schneider (1997a) on chaos theory as a possible model for dialect variability and change. A few references in passing on the possible suitability of chaos theory can be found in work by Mufwene (2001), Lightfoot (1991), and others – in very general terms. Mufwene (2008:131) states, without further contextualization or argumentation, that "Idiolects are 'complex adaptive systems,'" in line with his view of language varieties as produced by processes of competition and selection. Diane Larsen-Freeman has been a pioneer in applying this theory in many publications (e.g. Larsen-Freeman 1997, 2018b), operating from an applied, acquisition-based perspective, with a focus on learners' performance and learning processes rather than target languages as objects (Larsen-Freeman & Cameron 2008:7–11). Similarly, Nick Ellis has contributed interesting psycholinguistic work along these lines (e.g. Ellis 2008, 2011).[24] In general, CDS thinking is fairly well established in second-language acquisition linguistics, with a strong center

---

[23] For example, he (rightly, I think) explains the evolution of dialects and languages as emergent processes motivated by the fact that they "induce boundaries of trust, making a distinction between 'us' and 'them'" (Holland 2014:57, 90).

[24] Han (2019) applies the learner perspective of CDSs to the analysis of a corpus of email exchanges. See also Ortega & Han (2017), a festschrift for Diane Larsen-Freeman.

in Groningen (de Bot et al. 2007; Verspoor et al. 2008; de Bot et al. 2012; Verspoor 2012). Conceptual parallels with usage-based linguistics are most explicitly stated as such in Bybee's (2010) book, which discusses some similarities and explicitly has a chapter on "Language as a Complex Adaptive System."

To my knowledge, the earliest volume to claim the relationship with complex systems in its title is Larsen-Freeman & Cameron's (2008), which argues from a strongly applied perspective, suggesting the relevance of this approach for language teaching and acquisition. Ellis & Larsen-Freeman (2009) explicitly posit *Language as a Complex Adaptive System*, including a programmatic "position paper" by Beckner and colleagues (2009) which goes back to a meeting hosted by the Santa Fe Institute, called "Language Is A Complex Adaptive System": "The study of Complex Adaptive Systems, Emergentism, and Dynamic Systems Theory is a relatively recent phenomenon, yet it is revolutionizing our understanding of the natural, physical, and social worlds" (Ellis & Larsen-Freeman 2009:vi). The contributions in these books survey core properties of complexity and chaos which determine language behavior as well, but they do so in rather general terms (presenting theoretical deliberations with hardly any structural examples) and, again, from a strongly applied perspective (highlighting the relevance of this approach for language teaching and acquisition). Kretzschmar (2015), after a thematically related precursor volume (Kretzschmar 2009), also presents CDS theory explicitly as an alternative view to determinism and reductionism, considering the status of linguistics as a science. His work, which discusses a number of exciting ideas motivated by CDS thinking and relationships to neighboring disciplines, is strongly inspired by quantitative observations on data distributions in the American Linguistic Atlas, the "A-curve," power-law distributions of token-type relationships in atlas responses discussed in Section 4.3.7. Burkette and Kretzschmar's (2018) work is essentially the first introduction to linguistics that builds upon CDS principles, albeit also in very general, abstract terms. Hiver and Al-Hoorie (2019) offer an introduction to research methods appropriate for studying applied linguistic issues in a CDS perspective (and to the theory itself), explaining seven qualitative and seven quantitative methodological procedures. Mauranen (2017, 2018), Larsen-Freeman (2018a), and Vetchinnikova (2017) have related complex systems theory to ELF usage. Schneider (2020b, 2020c) offered sample applications of CDS thinking to historical and ongoing processes in English; Schmid (2020:340–41) implicitly posits it as an underlying theory. Lund and colleagues (2022) offer a broad but also rather abstract proposal along the same lines, highlighting aspects such as epistemological plurality, pragmatics, discourse practices, semiotic systems, cultural approaches, interaction, or multimodality.

Larsen-Freeman and Cameron (2008:16) point out a few core characteristics of a CDS approach as opposed to conventional modes of language analysis:

- emphasis on change and processes rather than static entities
- lack of clean data: "We expect data to be noisy and messy because the dynamics of complex systems produce variability"
- emphasis on context, which is "seen as an intrinsic part of a system, not as a background against which an action takes place"
- rejection of cause-effect explanations, to be replaced by processes of self-organization and emergence.

While all these authors, and a few more, consider CDS theory as a suitable approach for languages, it still seems clear that CDS thinking in linguistics constitutes largely a niche today. The applicability of the theory has been intuitively sensed, projected, and suggested, but it still needs to be expanded and filled with life. There has been no application to the emergence of WEs so far.

3 Turning Complex Dynamic Systems Theory into Linguistic Reality: The Central Role of Usage and Constructions

This discussion of CDS principles may sound rather abstract and general; the question is how these principles can be "translated" to down-to-earth manifestations in language, can be brought to life. I am firmly convinced that the "missing link" between the CDS theory and the specific properties of human languages and language varieties such as WEs is provided by the schools of usage-based linguistics and construction grammar. Both represent mainstream approaches today, opposed to abstract generativism, and on both disciplines extensive literature is available.

For the usage-based, functional paradigm, I recommend Bybee's (2010) work as an insightful introduction and survey, Diessel's (2017) as a concise, accessible introduction, Schmid's (2020) as a monumental but highly dense and technical survey that covers almost every conceivable aspect in a most convincing, thorough fashion, and Diaz-Campos and Balasch's (2023) as a comprehensive, authoritative handbook. Kretzschmar (2015:ch. 3) traces the relationship between usage-based linguistics and complex adaptive systems approaches through several core publications (though he ultimately blames these linguists for carrying on "old baggage from formal linguistics," 78).

A distantly related approach that combines fruitfully with usage-based thinking is the theory known as Construction Grammar, with the core notion of "constructions" defined as form-meaning pairings on various levels of concreteness (starting with individual lexical items) or abstractness (extending to "schematic" constructions conveying relational meanings between different lexical fillers). It builds upon work by Fillmore, Goldberg (2006), Croft, and many more. Hoffmann and Trousdale (2013) produced a monumental handbook; Hilpert (2019) and especially Hoffmann (2022) apply the concept in an accessible fashion to English grammar (see Hoffmann 2022:ch. 3 on the interaction of usage and constructions), just like Hilpert (2013) does for the history and development of the language. Laporte (2021) offers a comprehensive, impressive application study, working out "constructicons" (related sets of constructions) around the verb *make* in several WEs, tracing stages of conventionalization in some NEs. Ungerer and Hartmann (2023) discuss various approaches to the notion of constructions, also from a discipline-internal historical perspective and with reference to extant similarities to CDS thinking. They argue, for instance, that in sentences "the whole is more than the sum of its parts" (1), a statement also provided by Mitchell (2021) on CDSs in general (see also Section 2.2.2), that constructions constitute "a network of stored knowledge" (5), or can be understood as "emergent clusters" (8). Most importantly, Hoffmann (2021) suggests and documents that Construction Grammar offers a suitable cognitive explanation for the emergence of NEs as posited in the Dynamic Model (Schneider 2007).

Usage, the constant and perpetual flow of everyday utterances produced whenever humans interact, materializes language and keeps steering and modifying its character, constituents, and properties through its dual character as product (performance) and intake (reception). When we talk we encode functional, situation-specific needs and concepts, and choose between alternative ways of encoding a given message, drawing from a mentally stored set of meaning-form relations (words, constructions, patterns, or schemas) that the members of a speech community share (largely, though never completely, since each individual's experience has been unique). And at the same time, through producing these utterances, we contribute to, influence, and subtly modify the linguistic relations and habits stored in our interactants' minds, exposed to our utterances, just like we process and integrate language items and schemas we hear from others into our own mental knowledge system. Language (i.e. components of shared linguistic knowledge and habits as to sound-meaning-interrelations in specific situations) is thus a continuously enacted interplay of language production and perception in usage. The decisive processes in this are on the individual level entrenchment (relationships which are increasingly reinforced and hard-wired in one's synapses through frequent repetition) and, on the community level, conventionalization (the growth of shared connections and associations across community members through regular interaction between them). Schmid (2020) provides an intricately comprehensive and detailed account of these processes.

The perspective adopted by the usage-based paradigm is ultimately functional, assuming that language properties are shaped by communicative functional needs. Consequently, context is of major importance – both intralinguistic co-text (co-occurring items and constructions which help to encode and decode the message) and the extralinguistic context of situation, which also often clarifies situation-bound communicative needs, intended meanings. Some forms and schemes are abstract and usable in very many different ways and settings (e.g. the comparative correlative construction, as in *the more she slept the happier she felt*; *the richer a man is the bigger his car is* [Hoffmann 2022:230]), while others are strongly conventionalized ways of encoding intentions in specific contexts. Take *Good morning!* or *One for the road!* as examples of formally conventionalized utterances tied to very specific sociocultural settings – on hearing them we know, without further explanation, quite accurately what time of day it is, and what the circumstances are likely to be. Understanding, manipulating and integrating utterances in usage is assumed to build strongly upon domain-general cognitive principles (like perception, categorization, fore-/back-grounding, metaphor, analogy, embodiment, simplification, complexification, and so on); the school is rooted in decades of work in cognitive linguistics (Geeraerts & Cuyckens 2012; Xu Wen & Taylor 2021). It is also supported by what we know, increasingly, about its physiological realization (Schumann 2017): associations between concepts, utterance types, and structural schemes are hardwired through the build-up of neural connections between synapses in different regions of the brain ("neurons that fire together wire together"), and these connections are continuously strengthened through repetition (cf. Bossomeier 2000; Gerstner et al. 2014). Frequency of occurrence of forms, patterns, and associations thus plays an important role: entrenchment in individuals is continuously strengthened and associations are increasingly memorized and engrained through repetition. Conversely, on the community level the growth and spread of shared individual associations builds common language knowledge through conventionalization (see Schmid 2020 for detailed discussions of both entrenchment and conventionalization).

Consequently, such associations between functional, contextual needs and conventionalized expressions build incrementally through the perpetual wheel of interaction and usage, in much the same way CDSs evolve and continuously manifest themselves through time and space. Equivalent to the build-up of hierarchical complexity leading to emergence and auto-organization, in language, conventionalized, commonly licensed utterance and pattern/scheme types evolve and become established increasingly firmly (but may of course also be dissolved though the same type of processes in time). The continuous replication of these linguistic habits also allows for minute modifications in this process: for specific, local reasons or also just as products of some degree of random variability utterances produced by some individual somewhere sometime may contain slight alternations of whatever kind and thus introduce minute deviations and innovations, not (yet) licensed utterance types. While many of such deviations will go unnoticed and leave no traces, some, for whatever reasons, may catch on in the community, be picked up, become entrenched, and be replicated by others (i.e. become embryonic stages of language change on the community level). The usage-based school thus offers a reasonable and transparent account of the omnipresence of linguistic variability and change.

Such modifications, the cradle of change, may happen in interactions between adults and may come from some hidden corner in the community (any of the many variants in the "long tail" of Kretzschmar's [2015] "A-curve" may come to life and start gaining ground, for instance). It may also occur, however, in the transmission of linguistic habits and associations across generations, from caregivers to infants, whose brains and linguistic abilities at a young age are yet more flexible and open to strengthening slightly alternate realizations, reinterpretations of the input, and restructuring. It is noteworthy and important that the usage perspective also provides a succinct and convincing explanation of the process of language acquisition, which also operates incrementally through gradual and increasing copying, abstracting analysis, and entrenchment of outside linguistic input. As Tomasello (2003) showed, infants go through characteristic steps of acquisition that can be explained convincingly as gradual build-up and expansion of associations, abstractions, and the growth of an utterance inventory. Through constant interaction and co-operation, with caregivers and infants beginning to share joint attention frames, children first acquire "intention-reading" (triggering the insight that sounds symbolize meaningful information in life) and then gradually expand their ability to manipulate components of language via "holophrases" (single words expressing a complex idea), "pivot schemas" (two-word utterances consisting of a firm pivot item and another word in a variable slot) and more elaborate patterns to a full understanding of construction types and schemes. Obviously, this view challenges the generative belief in an innate abstract system of grammatical rules: "Linguistic experience – not grammar – is key to becoming a competent language user" (Christiansen & Callens 2022:4; see Archangeli & Pulleyblank 2022 for a similar claim on emergent phonology).

To put it pointedly, thus, "language" in this school is understood as shared associations and conventions on regular correlations between situation-grounded meanings and conventionalized utterance types, established and shared (with some potential for variability) among members of a speech community through conventionalization and engrained in individual minds via entrenchment (Schmid 2020). The notion of "grammar" grasps and describes these associations, characteristically with a focus on the strongest and most regular ones of these associations: Grammars establish "rules," describing common and conventionalized patterns, and they disregard linguistic creativity and the potential for both deviance and innovation. As DuBois (1985) once put this, "Grammars code best what speakers do most" (362; similarly Kretzschmar 2015:ch. 4). But there is always a potential for rarely-occurring or unlicensed sideline forms (possibly produced in acquisition processes or through transfer effects in multilingual settings), for variability, innovation, and change, possibly with a Darwinian component of certain constraints and probably also chance deciding which innovations survive. Some become established (and freshly conventionalized and entrenched), while many others vanish. And this is where WEs also come in, with locally distinct forms and structures (constructions) emerging and becoming conventionalized in a given region.

4 Complex Dynamic Systems Theory as Applied to World Englishes

4.1 On the Nature of World Englishes: Essentialist and Non-essentialist Reflections

For a long time, theorizing on WEs has tended to view these varieties as firm and distinct entities, nation-based and rooted in a territory, independent from (though related to) their donor varieties. This is the "essentialist" perspective of viewing language varieties as discrete, standalone and simply existing entities. Consequently, varieties were assigned to one of Kachru's "Three Circles" (Kachru 1985, 1992), and possibly (perhaps less straightforwardly) to one of the five developmental phases posited in the "Dynamic Model" (Schneider 2003, 2007).

On the other hand, there has also been awareness that varieties come in wildly different types, depending on the social circumstances of their origin, and there are fuzzy types and fuzzy boundaries, questioning the traditional categorial view. There are "borderline varieties," for instance, which defy easy categorization. Görlach (1996), in an entertaining paper entitled "And is it English?," showcased and discussed "utterances which are only marginally English" (171). In a similar vein, Mesthrie and Bhatt (2008) posited the existence not of simply "the English language" but of an "English Language Complex," distinguishing twelve different "variety types," including "Hybrid Englishes," "Jargon Englishes," and more.

And this trend toward recognizing linguistic fluidity, overlaps, fuzziness, and a lack of clear entities and boundaries has gained momentum in the last decade or so. In recent research on WEs, linguistic resources have increasingly been perceived as floating rather freely across time and space, being adopted and integrated in some contexts but unsuccessful in others. Well-known cases in point include Pennycook's "transnational flows" (2007), Blommaert's (2010) "sociolinguistics of globalization," or Meierkord's (2012) "interactions across Englishes." New, communicatively successful language constellations grow in "grassroots" contexts, far from the impact of prescriptive norming processes (Schneider 2016a, Meierkord & Schneider 2021), and mixed varieties that freely combine forms and resources from various languages around are mushrooming (cf. Schneider 2016b and Canagarajah's notion of "translanguaging," 2013). An increasing number of scholars have actually come to question the focus upon national varieties and boundaries as discrete, clear-cut entities (see Seargeant and Tagg [2011] or Mair's [2013] work on the diffusion of Nigerian Pidgin in cyberspace). Today's linguistic realities, in WEs and elsewhere, rather suggest the importance of unbounded dynamic diffusion processes, with globally transmitted linguistic resources and configurations of various kinds. And in fact, given Labov's "uniformitarian principle" and all we know about the ubiquity of linguistic dynamism and contact (Hickey 2020; Schreier & Hundt 2013 for English) there is no reason to assume things would have been different at any other time or place. Take "transnational Korean English" as a recent example: As Rüdiger and Baratta (2025) show, English and Korean have increasingly mutually influenced each other, and the popularity of Korean music and films and the "hallyu" wave have spread Korean expressions globally.

Similarly, once-clear-cut boundaries between variety types have increasingly been questioned. This applies quite strongly to the distinction between second-language and foreign-language varieties, Kachru's (1985, 1992) "Outer" and "Expanding" circles. Buschfeld (2013) was among the first to suggest that ESL and EFL are in fact not distinct categories but points on a continuum, with varieties moving from one end to another depending on social circumstances. Buschfeld and Kautzsch (2017) developed this idea into their "extra- and intraterritorial forces" (EIF) model, applied more widely in their later work (Buschfeld and Kautzsch 2020); they build on the Dynamic Model (to which theirs is something like a "plug-in"), identify the same phases in all variety types, and suggest that developments are driven by a set of forces that operate across the board. Similarly, the large number of children in many countries across Asia and Africa acquiring English as their home and first language increasingly questions the distinction between ENL and ESL (the notion of "native speaker" had been discussed critically in the discipline for a long time anyhow). Buschfeld (2020) pursues this aspect empirically in a study of children's speech in Singapore, where by now more than half of all children grow up with English as their home language.

4.2 The Emergence of World Englishes through the Lens of the Evolution of Complex Dynamic Systems

The previous section (which could have been expanded, providing further references and arguments along the same lines) has shown that neither varieties nor variety types constitute clear-cut systems or entities. This is wholly in line with the earlier descriptions of CDSs, and with its usage-based application. Very few speakers these days stay put where they grew up; increasingly people travel and migrate, get in touch with other cultures and languages, and interact with them, exchanging modes of behavior, linguistic habits, and the like. Socially and linguistically, things are continuously in flux, and new constellations and formations emerge, being functional in and adapted to new contexts. The evolution of WEs can perfectly well be seen in this way, as a reflection of such sociohistorical processes and interactions.

WEs originally emerged during and after the period of colonization,[25] and the interplay of transmission with migration and innovation explains their similarity to but also departure from their erstwhile donor varieties. The precise usage conditions and input factors differed substantially from any one manifestation to the others, though the fundamental underlying pattern remains largely constant (cf. Schneider 2007). In the colonies new social mixtures of speakers from different walks of life came together. Originally, British speakers migrating to foreign lands in colonization brought their (different kinds of overlapping, not wholly identical) Englishes with them and re-rooted them. In these processes many locals acquired English (in its variant forms) and re-shaped and transformed it, producing new conglomerates of words, properties, features, constructions, and schemas that were perpetually re-enacted and thus increasingly adjusted and modified. Most importantly, the Indigenous populations contributed their own distinctive backgrounds to the emergent linguistic situations, including familiarity with their local language forms and patterns and cognitive effects resulting from the second-language learning context. Thus, new agents and new attributes and pieces of information kept entering the communicative CDS, and drove linguistic developments into new directions and toward novel outcomes of the

---

[25] I am aware of the fact that this is a loaded term today, with awareness having grown, rightly so, of the huge injustice, disrespect to indigenous cultures and also cruelties involved in this historical period and process.

perpetual wheel of usage. Central to these emergent developments were the continuous impact of creative processes such as koinéization (diminishing some differences between some individuals' habits), innovation (generating new associations and habits), language contact (potentially introducing associations originally shared with speakers from another linguistic community), language shift (with some sub-components in speakers' linguistic knowledge getting lost and others transferred into new environments), and so on (see Schneider 2007:99–112 for a discussion of factors effective in the emergence of new varieties).

Viewed from this perspective, WEs are thus not new linguistic systems distinct from their parent varieties but extractions, continuations, and components of an overarching CDS of "English(es)" that has been evolving over millenia, with some shared and some newly evolved, distinct properties, elements and subsystems associated with specific regions, social contexts, or situational settings. To varying extents and with varying input factors and contextual conditions this applies both to postcolonial varieties such as Indian, Singaporean, or Kenyan English (with colonization and migration serving as the triggers), having emerged in earlier centuries, and, in the recent past, nonpostcolonial varieties such as Japanese, Dutch, or Namibian English (with globalization, new and transnational communicative options and cyberspace serving as transmitters). Hence, while this may sound a bit surprising or even provocative to some, especially to conservative gatekeepers who in many countries still defend the idea that only Standard BrE is the only acceptable variety (and worthy target of education), I argue (and I am convinced) that all varieties of English, whether standard or nonstandard, whether British or postcolonial, whether relatively "pure" (i.e. low-contact, in the sense of Trudgill 2011) or mixed, have evolved from the fundamentally same evolutionary process, the perpetual wheel of motion of a CDS, and are thus functionally and structurally equal components of the same process.[26] In other words, not only RP or Standard AmE or South Africa's "Respectable" white variety but also, say, Ghanaian English, Zimbabwean English, Hong Kong English, Philippine English, and also Nigerian Pidgin and Jamaican Patwa (and many more) are equally legitimate offspring of Old English or Chaucer's language, components of the same CDS like branches of the same tree.

---

[26] One reviewer asked for the relationship between this process and the process described in the Dynamic Model (DM; Schneider 2007) of the evolution of postcolonial Englishes (which is not a core topic of this Element). The DM spells out similarities of variety evolution in a more narrowly defined, specific historical context and period. The view of varieties emergence through CDS principles is much more all-encompassing, meant to describe language evolution in very general terms (though for practical purposes in this Element its discussion is constrained to World Englishes).

4.3 Structural Properties of World Englishes as Manifestations of Complex Dynamic Systems Principles

CDS theory offers a generic and fundamental perspective on language evolution, a "meta-theory," projecting abstract principles and forces. There is a need to "translate" them, to "boil them down" to specific observations and investigations, to individual explanations of language change in (World) Englishes. In other words, the theory needs to be adopted, adapted, developed, specified, and filled with life from the perspectives of language variation and change, as well as language history and evolution. In an earlier publication (Schneider 2020c), I used the notion of "meanderings" as a vivid metaphor for how changes proceed in Englishes as a CDS, partly in a random, nondirectional fashion but partly also motivated by the impact of fundamental structuring principles, imposed by cognition, functional needs, social parameters, and so on. Structurally, this may include a range of observable processes across different varieties, including changes in the set of available forms (with some innovative ones appearing and some older ones disappearing in the course of time), changes in distributional principles (as to which forms are used in which contexts, and why), changes in frequency distributions and preferences of individual forms and patterns in specific contexts (a continuous waxing and waning), and changes in the formal expression of functions (e.g. modifications of the morphosyntactic marking of meaningful grammatical categories and relations). These processes may be partly motivated (e.g. by semantic categorizations or syntactic principles), and partly they appear to display random frequency fluctuations, but in any case we witness perpetually ongoing dynamism, in line with the principles that characterize CDS.

To bring my message home and fill it with life, in this extensive application chapter I show how the various CDS principles relate to the emergence of WEs and how they manifest themselves in specific traits and properties of individual varieties. I argue that speakers of English and other languages constitute the agents of a CDS, and their ongoing exchange of context-bound utterances serves as the nonlinear shaping and modification of linguistic attributes and objects which in such systems develop constellations of their own kind – which is what we find in some contexts in some WEs. In these constellations qualitatively new and potentially more powerful configurations (constructions, sound-meaning relations) can emerge – which then are perceived as characteristics of new varieties of English. Typically, for each of the core properties of CDS I present background considerations that make the effectiveness of the principle in focus plausible, I mention some features and properties that may be accounted for in this light, and in most instances I zoom in to one or two features in specific WEs where the impact of these effects can be showcased in some detail. All these processes will be richly illustrated by examples and discussions of earlier scholarly work framed in a new spotlight. Needless to say, the set of examples presented represents my own subjective selection, based on my knowledge, experiences, and earlier work. Given the richness of studies of phenomena in WEs, with thousands of pertinent publications, many other, additional examples could be provided in each category.

It should be noted that the assignment of linguistic examples to CDS principles obviously is not a one-to-one relation. The CDS properties interact with each other in multiple ways, and, correspondingly, individual linguistic phenomena are typically motivated by several factors jointly. I select one as the most salient and suitable one, but other effects could be added, so repeatedly I will offer cross-references to other principles, too.

It needs to be conceded that these application cases essentially remain on a metaphorical level: my discussions relate to principles and their applications, to examples and their explanations, but they lack mathematical rigor. However, this is the case with most other applications of CDSs in the social sciences[27] and some in the natural sciences as well. The only exception is mathematics itself – but all simulations of reality are precisely that, approximations; so this approach seems adequate for language as well. Usually there is a multitude of possible parameters which potentially influence any developmental trajectory, and most of them cannot be objectively measured and quantified, so a certain amount of leeway and abstraction in applications of the discipline seems unavoidable. For language, just as a thought experiment, we would need a full record of all utterances ever made in a speech community to be able to completely trace and model the spread of innovations and changes, the processes described and predicted by the CDS approach – and obviously this is completely out of the question. However, in World Englishes research, we have witnessed a strong trend toward increasingly sophisticated quantitative analyses (notably, various types of regression, conditional inference tress, and random forests) of huge electronic text corpora, which can be viewed as zooming in to fractions of the overall CDS tightly restricted in terms of time, place, and source; the efficacy of such studies in a CDS perspective remains to be addressed. Large-scale quantitative corpus studies can at best provide approximations to the working and understanding of CDS principles – valuable ones, though.

The alternative way of dealing with complexity emergence, more germane to CDS theorists and often practiced in the Santa Fe Institute, for instance, will be digital simulations – positing agents, attributes, and a starting setting and

---

[27] Take the extensive application of the notion of nonlinearity to a theory of political evolution in Brown (1995), for example. Also, see Larsen-Freeman & Cameron's (2008:11–15) defense of a metaphorical approach.

defining process rules applied step-by-step and recursively, checking whether what these constellations produce seems similar to observed reality. This would be a principled, formalistically rigid deductive procedure, considered scientifically valid but only mirroring, not operating upon reality; a possible direction toward the application of this line of thinking will be suggested in Section 5. My current approach, in contrast, is inductive and grounded in concrete linguistic observations. I hold that this is equally legitimate to mathematical formalisms or computational simulations, and it has the advantage of connecting theory with real-life linguistic forms and usage. Examples will be drawn from a wide range of linguistic publications (including some work of my own). I will also repeatedly refer to the systematic documentation of feature distributions in eWAVE (quoting feature numbers within that project, abbreviated as "f"), the *electronic World Atlas of Varieties of English* available online (ewave-atlas.org; Kortmann, Lunkenheimer & Ehret 2020). Clicking on feature names in eWAVE produces electronic maps that show the global distribution of the feature in question, also in different types of varieties (traditional or high-contact L1 dialects, indigenized L2s, and pidgins and creoles). Again, this will necessarily be somewhat selective – the vast majority of eWAVE features, resulting from basic CDS effects, could be assigned somewhere.

4.3.1 Systemness

The presence of systemic relations is obvious and uncontroversial in all kinds of varieties of English. As stated in Section 2.2.1, syntagmatic, co-occurrence relationships build larger units, and paradigmatic relations determine meaningful choices between functionally equivalent potential fillers of any slot. Here is a simple example from WEs, a prototypical structure found in Colloquial Singaporean English:

(1) *I dunno lah.* (from an informal conversation; source: Schneider 2020a: 169)

Even this simple three-word pattern allows us to identify a number of systemic language-internal relations between clause constituents of several kinds. The words represent a basic syntagmatic pattern (S-Aux-Neg-V-A$_{[sentence\ adverbial\ /\ discourse\ marker]}$). The "underlying" items *do* + *not* + *know* are syntagmatically fused to yield *dunno*. The (typically Singaporean) discourse marker *lah* takes a syntagmatic role as sentence adverbial modifying the matrix clause proposition, with specific semantics ('assertion'); and in itself it represents an actively selected element of a subsystem, potentially contrasting with further Singlish discourse markers such as *lor* (which would mean 'compromise'), *meh* (indicating 'uncertainty'), and others.

Systemic relations operate mainly within a given variety; across varieties they can be compared, and of course they can influence each other (in a network-like relationship) and they vary in terms of the complexity levels involved. An example of a subsystem that is ostensibly related to and only moderately more complex than the metropolitan one is the set of demonstratives and distinctions expressed by them. Mainstream English encodes a binary distinction of near vs. far relative to the speaker (*this/these* vs. *that/those*; see Section 4.3.5). Some dialects (e.g. on the Shetland and Orkney Islands) are moderately more complex by adding a third term, *yon*, meaning 'distant from both speaker and hearer' (Siemund 2013:96). A case of a quite different and much more complicated systemic set-up is the pronoun system of Bislama, an English-derived creole spoken in Vanuatu. Influenced by Indigenous languages (and thus also showing network complexity), Bislama distinguishes not only singular and plural but in addition has dual (for exactly two referents) and trial (for three) forms, and for all of them except the singular the variety distinguishes inclusive from exclusive forms (i.e. whether the addressee is included in the referent set or not). On the other hand, there is no distinction by gender or subject/object/possessive form. So, for example, *hem* is 'he', 'she', 'him', 'her', 'his', and so on; *yumitrifala*, the inclusive trial, means 'me, you, and somebody else', *mifala* (first person plural exclusive) means 'we (more than three, not including you)', and so on (see Siemund 2013:97).

Systemic and network relations are obviously also involved in functional reassignments of pronoun forms found rather widely (i.e. subject forms used as objects and vice versa, subject or object forms used as possessives, and various modifications of gender reference [eWAVE f1–2,5–6, 18–27, 29–31]). Very many varieties have developed distinct second person plural pronouns (thus resolving the ambiguity of standard English *you*) such as *y'all*, *youse*, *you'uns*, *you guys*, *unu*, and so on, thus also changing systemic relations in the set-up and meaning of pronouns. The same applies to other modifications of pronominal uses and relations in several WEs (e.g. the emergence of a distinction of inclusive versus exclusive non-singular first person pronouns [just shown for Bislama; eWAVE f36]), or various types of pro-drop (eWAVE f42–44). Over many centuries the relativization system of English has undergone fundamental systemic changes triggered partly by other reorganization processes in English. Examples include the intrusion of French-/Latin-derived *wh*-relativizers into a formerly invariant position (Old English *þe*, related to modern *that*), the reorganization of formal choices based on animacy (*who* vs. *which*), various constraints on omitting a relative pronoun ("gapping," acceptable in standard English in object and prepositional complement position [*the man I saw, the man I talked to*] but only in some dialects as a subject [*the man Ø talked to me helped me*]), the loss of case marking over time (cf. *whom* vs. object *who* and *whose* vs. *of which*), and more (Schneider 2020c). All of these processes interact and are realized and structured somewhat differently in WEs (see the documentation in eWAVE, f185–199), involving rearrangements based on underlying systemic relations, affecting the orderly character of partial systems, involving network relations, and often self-organization. For example, the genitive relativizer *of which*, as opposed to *whose*, is used substantially more frequently in Indian English (IndE) than in other varieties (Schneider 2020c:98). Developments increasing order (addressed in Section 4.3.5), such as regularization or the establishment of clear distinctions in demonstrative relations, also relate to and result from systemic pressures and tendencies.

4.3.2 Complexity

Language-externally, it seems reasonable to see speakers as the agents of a CDS, and their language production as associated attributes. Larsen-Freeman (2018a) mentions "individual human beings, their contact zones, and globalized networks" as relevant parameters (54). In line with CDSs, in WEs, as in all languages, there is an enormously large number of speakers who keep interacting, a prerequisite for complexity. Speakers are individuals and act as such, and the principle of local agency without a steering authority that is central to CDSs clearly applies: people speak with their family, friends, neighbors and other interaction partners, mostly (at least in informal contexts) without having communicative conventions on a larger social, say national, level in mind, but by doing so they inadvertently contribute to the conventionalization of the forms they use, and to language evolution. In addition, a level of social complexity results from the fact that they are embedded in, shaped by and actants of group relationships marked by sociolinguistic parameters, and also agents in sociopolitical processes, thus representing a higher-level order of conglomerates. Relevant individuals in WE-producing settings were, for example, Indigenous low-status people, members of established local elites, settler merchants, missionaries, and so on. Consequently, in addition to the myriad of individual input experiences and factors this also introduces some level of order, so the interactants' linguistic performance is not only to be seen as potentially chaotic idiolects but also as partly determined by levels of social organization, cooperation, and possibly low-level predictability. For example, specifically with respect to WEs, in the Dynamic Model of the evolution of Postcolonial Englishes (Schneider 2007), political factors determine identities of and changing relationships between settlers and Indigenous groups, and the sociolinguistic interactions between them are decisive for the process of "structural nativization," the emergence of locally characteristic language patterns, and the evolution of NEs – clearly processes with many agents, hierarchies, and levels of complexity involved. For example, local leaders and their sons (hardly ever daughters, I am afraid, in paternalistic social structures) were lured to associate with colonists in Britain's characteristic "indirect rule" leadership pattern and thus offered access to English schools and better acquisition of the language, while typically Indigenous workers and lower-class people had no such opportunity and acquired English not at all or in natural interaction contexts and in "grassroots" format (Schneider 2016a). Social organization thus was one of the major input factors that were instrumental in linguistic evolution and complexity emergence.

Equally, of course, there are all kinds of intra-linguistic network structures – mutual relations and similarities between linguistic forms and constituents of all kinds. As an example, let us look at the evolving functions of the form *one* in time and space. It started out in Old English as a plain numeral, and in the course of time it adopted a range of new functions including pronoun (*buy one*), determiner (*one person I know*), adjective (*her one concern*), and a noun phrase head substitution form sometimes called "propword," with specific semantic constraints of rejecting an attribute and replacing it by another (*an interesting book and a boring one*; Rissanen 1997; Schneider & Buschfeld 2020). Clearly, these functions relate to each other (and to other constituents in the same slots) in systematic and increasingly complex ways; and this trend continues into WEs. In Cyprus or Namibia, for example, *one* functions as a presentational indefinite article (*My sister is one art teacher*; Schneider & Buschfeld 2020:136). The most interesting and creative innovation, however, indicative of dynamism and network complexity, can be found in Colloquial Singaporean English, where *one* functions as something like a clause-final relativizer mirroring and modifying an underlying, motivating structure from Chinese (e.g. *those wear black one* 'the ones who wear black'; Bao 2015:104; see eWAVE f195). Gwee (2018), a book written entirely in "Singlish," abounds in such examples, including, apparently, some with wider functions: for example, "they last time got say 'chap-barang' one" (60); "this fella is ang moh pai one" (116); "words ... that can be used in so many ways one?" (143). The last example is particularly interesting from a network perspective since it obviously combines two distinct relativization strategies (which thus interact to reinforce each other rather than being mutually exclusive), English *that* and Singlish *one*.

An increase of complexity is also involved in the formation of multi-morpheme words (in word formation), chunking and phraseologisms described in Section 4.3.6, or in the growth of more variable schematic constructions shown by Hoffmann (2021; see Section 4.3.6).

4.3.3 Perpetual Dynamics

The relevance of this point is obvious, I think: The ongoing transmission of English from Old English times to the present day, mentioned earlier, comprises all elements of the "English Language Complex" (Mesthrie & Bhatt 2008:1–10). English has continuously been passed on (and partly been transformed in this process) to regional and colonial dialects, and in that sense, as mentioned earlier, "Singlish," IndE, Nigerian Pidgin English and all other NEs and contact varieties are equally continuations and dynamic re-instantiations of what once was Old or Middle English, daughter varieties of or complex interacting branches of this overall CDS of "English(es)"!

In addition to the examples of continuous diffusion (see Section 2.2.3), there is also always discontinuity (i.e. change, innovation, and the adoption of elements from contact languages). For example, Singlish has subject omission in *Can!*, IndE has the lexeme *dhoti*, and Nigerian Pidgin English has a second-person plural pronoun *una* – all "picked up" at some point along the way through time and space for some reason, and not shared by the others.

The perpetual dynamism of WEs as CDSs involves most immediately quantitative changes: in certain varieties some forms or patterns may become more frequent, in others they may fall into disuse. Kretzschmar (2015) rightly posits that "'change' in the complex system of speech will consist of an alteration in frequency of any particular feature, instead of the selection of one form over another" (113); and I would add that selection, one form winning out and an older one vanishing, may become a later option, thus with ultimately qualitative effects. In general, qualitative changes (new forms and schemes being introduced, like the ones mentioned in the previous paragraph) are also possible; and, as just stated, an interaction between both (when frequency differences gradually become so drastic that alternative choices in different varieties result) is another option. It is noteworthy that this applies to the relationship between the major metropolitan varieties, BrE and AmE, as well: While it is often posited that both are distinguished by clearly distinct choices (*petrol – gas, pavement – sidewalk*, etc.; nonrhotic vs. rhotic pronunciation of words like *car, card*; /aː/ vs. /æ/ in *dance*, etc.), Algeo (2006) showed that the vast majority of differences are quantitative in nature, with the same forms being used on both sides of the Atlantic but frequencies and preferences varying drastically in many instances (cf. Schneider 2025b).

Here is a small-scale but suggestive example of such an interaction between frequency fluctuation and the possibility of qualitative preferences shifting, regarding lexicosemantic change in IndE. I investigated interactions between word meanings and frequencies of words or word meanings in different varieties (see Schneider 2020b), and I found emerging strong preferences in some varieties. For example, let us look into the meanings expressed by the verb *learn*. I posit there are three core meanings: 'receive information' (*I learned you had an accident*), 'store information' (*I learned some Malay words*), and 'acquire an ability' (*Suzy learned how to swim*). In IndE we can observe change based on data from the 1970s (the "Kolhapur Corpus") and from around 2000 (the ICE corpus component). As Figure 3a shows, in those roughly two decades the core meaning 'store information' gained ground quite strongly (from 206 out of 258, i.e. 79.8% of all tokens to 325/381, i.e. 85.3%), while both other meanings remained roughly constant in frequency. It is noteworthy that in all ESLs in that study the proportion of this core meaning is higher than in BrE (though not as prominently as in India), which suggests that in the transmission into NEs a "focusing" process seems to be going on, favoring the further growth of dominant variants at the expense of weaker ones, which may be falling into disuse over time. Similar developments and shifting preferences were observed with frequency relationships between near-synonyms. For example, *assume* and *suppose* denote roughly the same mental process, but in India, much more than

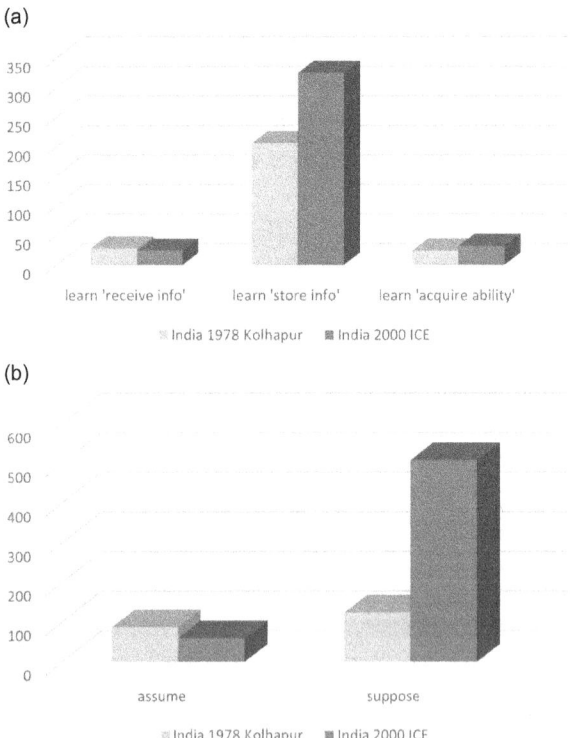

Figure 3a and 3b Shifting frequencies of preferred meanings and lexical choices in India, 1978 vs. ~2000. After Schneider (2020b:36, 34).

elsewhere, *suppose* has come to be the preferred lexeme: In the Kolhapur corpus *suppose* occurs only moderately more frequently than *assume* (124 versus 87 tokens, i.e. 58.8% of the sum of both), but some twenty years later it predominates strongly (508 over 59 tokens, =89.6%), with *assume* having become substantially dispreferred (see Figure 3b).

Bernaisch's (2015) study of Sri Lankan English documents a wide range of lexicogrammatic properties and innovations that are mainly characterized by significant frequency preferences, and consequently the author discusses norm issues, the question of how much difference in frequency is required to claim endonormativity (376), or the emergence of structural profiles indicative of a semiautonomous status (ch. 6).

In Section 2.2.3 I illustrated the ongoing dynamism in the evolution of English by outlining shifts and changes in the sub-system of modal verbs. This story can easily be continued by following it up into WEs, where the permanent quantitative fluctuation and ongoing processual readjustments between individual forms can equally be found. In regional Inner-Circle (L1) dialects, alternative options and properties to the developments in Standard English have been retained or have emerged. For example, in Southern AmE double modals can be found (e.g. *I might could do that*), in a pattern which violates the modern English rule of allowing only one modal in a clause. However, this may be seen as continuing the Old English property of being able to combine preterite presents in the same predication, with special pragmatic functionality (e.g. implying tentativeness). In WEs, frequency shifts of modal usage are common; for example, *shall* occurs very frequently in Kenya but is rare in Hong Kong (Collins & Yao 2012). Hansen (2018) provides a comprehensive investigation of variation and change in modal verbs in three second-language NEs (from Hong Kong, India, and Singapore, based on ICE corpus data and bringing in a sociolinguistic perspective, most importantly via an apparent-time methodology), focusing on the domain of obligation and necessity. She shows, for example, that in Hong Kong *have to* is used most frequently, with quite some difference, by younger speakers aged 17–25, and that the root (obligation) meaning of *must* decreases sharply through all age cohorts (272–73; similarly in India, 281). All varieties, most strongly India, use *must* commonly to express epistemic modality (307). As a strong causal factor she identifies "profound influence of the substrate languages" (309). In general, she finds consistent frequency differences of uses of specific modals (e.g. the semi-modal *have to*) across varieties (310–11). The ESL varieties are shown to follow native varieties in some core trends, notably the decrease of core modals (especially deontic *must*) and an increase of some semi-modals, especially *have to* (less so *have got to* and *need to*). In a similar vein (and looking into the same varieties), Laporte (2021) shows how different varieties come to prefer different constructions involving the core verb *make*, and she points out frequency-based emerging syntactic, lexical and semantic idiosyncracies in the NEs investigated (298).

So, it's a *perpetuum mobile*, a continuous reshuffling process with old forms retaining old properties only in some varieties but gaining new functions in others, with the frequency of individual forms waxing and waning from one variety to another, with relations constantly changing in a process that never ends.

4.3.4 Network Relations

In Section 2.2.4, I argued that the notion of network in languages can be regarded as applying in an extralinguistic and an intralinguistic perspective.

In the language-external perspective, speakers are agents with specified network relations between them, and interactions between them manifest network behavior. In the so-called "second wave" of variationist sociolinguistics the concept of social networks became crucially integrated into the discipline's thinking in work by Jim and Lesley Milroy in Belfast, which explicitly showed that speech behavior and language forms used depended on speakers' networks, their communication patterns and interaction habits (Milroy 1980). Similarly, interaction patterns between locals and colonists as described in the Dynamic Model of Postcolonial Englishes (Schneider 2007; see Section 4.3.2) constitute networks of various degrees of density, and the unilateral implication between factors such as politics, identities, interaction patterns and, consequently, constructions establishes a complex network dependency leading from external conditions to internal structural properties.

Language-internally, many interrelationships and mutual or unilateral causal dependencies between specific constructions can also be identified. Consider my earlier example introduced in Section 2.2.4, the longitudinal change of character of English from synthetic to analytic, which involved a large-scale loss of endings throughout its history. It can be readily shown that today in some WEs (e.g. China English) this trend continues further: the *-s* suffix on verbs (for the third person singular) or nouns (for plural) is often omitted (Schneider 2011). This is obviously due to substrate effects of analytic Sinitic languages: Mandarin Chinese lacks endings for verb concord or noun pluralization, and this linguistic habit remains to some extent when Chinese people acquire and speak English. We are confronted with a crosslinguistic network relationship here: a morphosyntactic property of Chinese relates to and interferes with Chinese speakers' language production in English.

An impressive example of such a crosslinguistic, typologically motivated network relation is offered by the work of Brunner (2017). The author convincingly documents a strong typological effect of local Indigenous languages on the emerging structural choices in noun phrases in the Englishes of Singapore and Kenya. Notably, such a connection would not be sensed by speaker intuition but surfaces only with the help of a rigorous quantitative methodology, although it is shown to be robust and highly statistically significant. Asian substrate languages in Singapore (Baba Malay, Hokkien, Mandarin, and Cantonese) are predominantly head-final, while the East African Bantu, Nilotic, and Cushitic languages in Kenya are characterized by a head-initial character and postnominal dependents. As the author shows (Brunner 2017:170–205), this preference gets transferred in a network-like relation to the emerging regional Englishes: in Singaporean English premodifiers within the noun phrase occur more prominently and tend to be longer and internally more complex (Example 2a), while in Kenyan English postmodifiers are found more frequently, with the same formal properties (Example 2b).

(2) (a) a four month kind of attachment (ICE-SIN; Brunner 2017:180)
    (b) any barrier hindering you from that kind of marriage (ICE-EA; Brunner 2017:191)

Thus, network relations between structural associations based on Indigenous Asian and African languages, respectively, extend to emerging linguistic habits in the evolution of Singaporean and Kenyan English, respectively, and in a most subtle manner affect speakers' associations and habits in these varieties.

Another example of emerging, expanding, and changing language-internal network relations is provided by the innovative spread of "intrusive *as*" especially in IndE (and also, less well established, in other South Asian Englishes), as documented by Lange (2016) and Koch and colleagues (2016; see also Schneider 2020b). As these authors show (see Example 3, from Lange 2016), in complex transitive verb complementation structures (Quirk et al. 1985), where verbs are followed by an object and an object complement which classifies the object (as in *I consider her my advisor*), a connecting particle *as* has become established in IndE and South Asian Englishes with verbs that do not allow this construction in metropolitan varieties.

(3) The main temple is called as Rang-Mahal.
    a teacher named as Mr. Keating

It has been shown that this construction occurs most commonly in IndE, less frequently in other South Asian Englishes (notably Sri Lanka), and also elsewhere, especially in learners' utterances; and in IndE it is associated most effectively with certain verbs that commonly occur with it (mainly t*erm as*, *call as, name as*). This is a complex, perhaps even strange construction, since the word class of *as* in this pattern is by no means clear, even counterintuitive: It can be viewed as a preposition or a conjunction, but in fact in these constructions it expresses, surprisingly, "a copular relation" (Quirk et al. 1985: 1200), a "predicative" function (Aarts 1992), since *I regard him as my friend* corresponds to a relation prototypically expressed by a copula (cf. *I think he is my friend*; cf. Schneider 1997b). The point is that this construction has a source model in standard English (*I consider/regard him as my friend*), but only with a small set of verbs, being barred from this structure with many other, semantically identical or similar ones (**I think/believe him as my friend*). Now, whatever the reason (forces of analogy, an increase of transparency, contact-induced origins, etc.), it is clear that new associations have been built (between this construction type and verbs suitable for it), at varying degrees of strength in India, South Asia, and elsewhere, and network connections between words, structural meanings, and construction types are being built and expanding, producing slightly more complex and ever-evolving systemic relations.

A simpler example of a network relationship plainly between formal constituents is the inventory of reflexives found across varieties of English. The forms of Standard English are somewhat erratic – for instance, *myself* is derived from the possessive pronoun *my* but *themselves* from the personal pronoun object form *them*. In WEs, all kinds of combinations, both of personal and possessive stems in different persons and of *-self/-selves* independent of number, and also just simple forms, occur (e.g. *meself, hisself, ourself, theirself, him*, etc.); for documentation, see Siemund (2013:26–33; eWAVE f11–16). All these constituents and relations are thus connected with each other as network elements, showcasing a lot of creative potential.

Obviously, some of the other structures discussed in this Element involve network relations as well, for example the Malaysian/Singaporean English *kena* passive, which affects the paradigmatic relationship with passive formations with *be* or *get* (see Section 4.3.5), or the different emerging constructions around the core verb *make* documented by Laporte (2021). Other cases in point, which also relate to systematicity and complexity, are pronoun uses in widened functions, such as *she/her* or *he/him* for inanimate referents or generalized subject or object pronoun forms (eWAVE f1–2, 5–6) or the well-known alternation (and prescriptivist discussions about it) between *me* and *I* (*John and me/I*) in coordinate subjects (eWAVE f7).

4.3.5 The Interplay of Order and Chaos

Broadly, "ordered" relations can be understood as sets of a small number of choices with clear functional assignments, while chaotic relations involve a large number of entities with unpredictable properties and modes of behavior. An example from the evolution of English which remains effective in WEs, of course, was briefly characterized in Section 2.2.5 – the breakdown of a once orderly system of functionally predictable verb forms as opposed to today's co-existence of many irregular verb forms.

A rather simple example with effects in WEs is the relation between the simple past verb form (*I wrote*) and the present perfect (*I have written*). In standard BrE (Quirk et al. 1985) the former marks an event as completed, having occurred at some point in the past, whereas the perfect implies some sort of ongoing current relevance for the present moment of time (with the activity in question being ongoing, recent with immediate effects on the present situation, or having occurred within a time frame that spans up to now). This systematic relation (order as a firm form-meaning implication) became established during the Early Modern English period, very roughly between the sixteenth and the eighteenth centuries, so in postcolonial varieties which branched off during that period, including AmE, it is known to be less firmly established as a grammatical habit (Werner 2014; Werner et al. 2016; cf. Siemund 2013:115–16, eWAVE f99–100). Predictable implications between structure and meaning, as in standard BrE, can be understood as orderly relations, while variable, fuzzy relations, where it is not clear what exactly a perfect or past structure entails, represent a step toward a chaotic set-up.

A similar relationship obtains with another grammatical feature of English which historically is fairly young, the distinctive function and meaning of the progressive (*She is running*.) While in metropolitan English the progressive clearly marks an activity as ongoing, incomplete, and viewed from inside (as opposed to the simple form which implies an outside perspective on a completed or stative fact), it is well known that in NEs the progressive is used more widely, also for stative predications (*I am knowing that. She is owning a car*; for documentation, see Siemund 2013:138–40, eWAVE f88). The effect is the same as described in the previous paragraph: an orderly relationship, with a specific form signaling a distinctive meaning, is dissolved, so the overall system, the syntax-semantics interface, becomes a little more unpredictable and chaotic.

As a further example of the oscillation between orderly and chaotic properties (involving other CDS principles as well), let us have a short look at the discourse particles of Colloquial Singapore English, which have been widely investigated and documented (e.g. Lim 2004:5.3). Singlish is known to have an abundance of such forms, which denote varying attitudes to the proposition expressed (which then is implied to be evident, annoying, surprising, etc.), beginning with the ubiquitous and generally well-known *lah* particle (*Can, lah!*). These items have been borrowed over decades from various regional donor varieties like Baba Malay, Hokkien, or Cantonese, and the set of such forms has been continuously expanded and integrated into the same grammatical slot of discourse markers (Lim 2007): speakers of Singlish know that items such as *meh, lor, hor,* and others, often in clause-marginal positions, are "subjective comments" on the statement made, expressing a personal stance toward it. This associative, by now stable grammatical knowledge conventionalized among Singlish speakers constitutes an element of order in this variety: Speakers know how to interpret these forms in context, they understand that by using them their interlocutors subtly express a stance, position themselves relative to their utterance. And this is a young, recently emerged pocket of order: It is known that these particles have emerged over the last few decades, together with the growth of Singlish as a distinct marker of a local cross-cultural identity. This orderly relation serves as an attractor, since it integrates other forms and expressions, and in this process affects and streamlines their usage condition. For example, Wee (2003) showed that the single form *know*, derived and shortened from the English parenthetical *you know*, has been pulled and integrated into this discourse marker slot, and it now functions increasingly like other monosyllabic discourse markers. And the set of such forms is productive and open to expansion, which adds a slightly "chaotic," potentially destabilizing option to the partial system. A relatively recent addition to the Singlish set of discourse markers is the form *sia*, for instance (Hieramoto et al. 2022).

A specific manifestation of chaotic systems, referred to in Section 2.2.5, are the so-called "catastrophies" described by Thom, and among these in particular the phenomenon of bifurcation – the case that a single entity splits into two (i.e. either one form develops two functions or one function comes to be expressed by two different formal means).

An example of the former process is the emergence of locally distinctive, innovative functions of the forms *only* and *itself* in IndE as focus markers (Bernaisch & Lange 2012; Lange 2012). The form *only* in IndE has developed a novel function called "presentational," placed immediately after the constituent (mostly noun phrase) that it focuses on (Sailaja 2009:55; see Figure 4). Since this innovation has not dispensed the older, original use it may thus have one of two different functions and meanings, either the distinctively Indian presentational one (as in Example 4a and Figure 4) or the mainstream "contrastive" one (as in Example 4b) – it "does double duty as contrastive and as presentational focus marker " (Lange 2012:185). Similarly, the form *itself* has evolved into an intensifying focus marker following its referent, which, unlike in other varieties of English, need not be a noun phrase but can, for example, be an adverbial, as in

Figure 4 Example of presentational use of *only* in IndE (from Mehrotra 1998:115). Reprinted with permission.

(Example 4c). As Bernaisch & Lange (2012) show, this presentational, focus-marking function of *itself* has also spread to other South Asian Englishes (see also Lange 2012:193–95), and it is possibly motivated by functionally similar focus particles in South Asian languages, thus building crosslinguistic network relations.

(4) (a) These women only said this. (Sailaja 2009:55)
    (b) I saw only him [not anybody else].
    (c) you should start going to the gym from now itself (Lange 2012:186).

Another example of a case of bifurcation, starting from a functional category, can be selected from the grammar of Singaporean English (similarly in Malaysian English). In standard English the passive is built by a form of *be* plus a past participle (*The mail was delivered*); alternatively (more informally and less commonly) *be* can be replaced by *get* as an auxiliary, implying a stronger component of suffering from the activity expressed (*John got beaten*). Singlish has borrowed an additional passive auxiliary from Malay, *kena*, which carries additional semantic constraints: The activity expressed by a *kena*-passive must be something unpleasant that the subject undergoes involuntarily. An example from a Singlish conversation between young males is *he kena play out* ('he was cheated'; Schneider 2020:170, 172). The Singlish book mentioned earlier (Gwee 2018) also offers a number of examples of this construction, such as "Poor guy kena whacked a lot" (38); "you kena influenced by ang moh culture" (112). The semantic space of passivity is thus subdivided in a novel way in that variety, introducing a new level of complexity (and order/lack of order) when compared to metropolitan English.

Stenroos (2008) documents another instance of "order [emerging] out of chaos" in a historical phase of BrE dialect. The loss of grammatical gender between Old and Middle English is generally assumed to have resulted in "confusion" (445). The author subscribes to the variationist axiom "that linguistic variation is, on the whole, orderly rather than chaotic" (446), assuming that orderly, systematic patterns are "in principle describable, even though they may be very complex" (446) – fully in line with CDS principles as applied and understood in this Element. Based on thirteenth-century texts from the Southwest Midlands, she shows that in that specific domain the assignment of new pronominal gender reference followed semantic distinctions based on animacy, individuation and natural categorizations. Thus, again we witness a semantically motivated reorganization from an orderly stage via a moderately turbulent transition period to the establishment of newly orderly notional distinctions.

Actually, a look into the history of English offers another beautiful example of the oscillation between orderly and chaotic sub-systems; many grammars of Old and Middle English touch upon this phenomenon, but McColl Millar (2000) traces and documents it in exemplary detail (and also through standard and nonstandard sub-varieties). Old English had a complex but fundamentally orderly system of articles/demonstratives, with a very large number of different forms, depending upon whether the form was "simple" or "compound" (i.e. unmarked or the demonstrative act enforced), and then varying by three genders, four cases, and to some extent different noun classes and regions. By the end of the Old English period this set of forms and their functional assignments broke down completely (perhaps due to contact with Scandinavian languages), so for a while this development seems to have resulted in pure chaos in the identification of a noun phrase referent. But, remarkably, toward Middle English a new, beautifully orderly system of an article (*the*) and only four demonstratives emerged, distinguishing only two parameters (proximity, i.e. near vs. far to the speaker, and number, i.e. singular vs. plural), expressed by *this – that/these – those*, respectively. Interestingly enough, these individual forms all can be traced back to forms that had existed in the Old English system (with totally different functions), so fragments from an earlier system survived the in-between chaos and were reassigned new functions in an emerging new pattern of order. In a wider perspective, see the large number of features in eWAVE involving interchanges or functional reassignments of articles, determiners, and demonstratives, all, of course, somehow affecting systemic and network relations and thus also the amount and character of order in a given variety (eWAVE f59–71).

Regularization may be seen as a product of systemic pressure toward orderly relations – e.g. of noun plural formation (*childrens*, *sheeps*; eWAVE f48) or of verb past tense forms (like *gived*, *knowed*; Section 2.2.5).

4.3.6 Emergentism and Self-Organization

An example from English dialects illustrates the emergence of systematically organized subsystems through time: Anderwald's (2001) work on an emerging polarity-based systemic opposition in past tense copula forms in dialects of BrE (based on the 10 million-word corpus of spoken colloquial English which is part of the British National Corpus [BNC]). Her starting point is the observation that the past tense forms of the English copula (*was – were*) show an irregular, unusual distribution, with the choice of a verb form based on the grammatical person of the subject, different from the behavior of main verbs (*I was – you(sg.) were – she was – we/you(pl.)/they were*). This is a case of irregularity without a function (a residual trace of an earlier language stage), and as such, thus, prone to be removed.

A simple "solution," found in many dialects, is the choice of a single form throughout all grammatical persons – most likely the majority form *was*, which yields *I/you/she/we/they was* – a pattern which is common in some dialects (e.g. African American Vernacular English or Southern AmE). However, the relationship gets more complex when polarity, commonly expressed by phonologically weak morphological clitics (-*n't*), comes in. Anderwald's analysis shows that positive *was* but negative *weren't* are spreading in all grammatical persons in BrE dialects (the same tendency has been documented for the dialect of the island of Ocracoke, NC; Wolfram & Schilling-Estes 1997:83–84). Since this is an unexpected, counterintuitive result it is worth asking why this is the case. The new distribution marks positive versus negative polarity (the important piece of information of "yes or no?") not only by the (phonetically weak) clitic –*n't* but strengthens it by distinct stem choices added: *was* always signals positive information, *were* marks negative propositions. In other words, this ongoing reorganization of a formal subsystem in BrE dialects marks priority given to the distinct expression of polarity over the traditional, synchronically unmotivated English person-number system. Clearly this can be interpreted as an evident self-organizing tendency in BrE dialects, based on the strength and impact of cognitive factors and principles, and also as a process introducing a small pocket of order (formal consistency based on polarity) into what in standard English is a slightly erratic (chaotic?) paradigm.

Emergence and auto-organization manifest themselves also in the construction of new, complex entities, either in word formation (Biermeier 2008) or by chunking, the formation of multi-word items or "prefabs." In Outer Circle WEs, on the lexical level new complex entities have been produced (i.e. local, partly patterned word formation products). We find new compounds (e.g. IndE *chai wallah, rikshaw wallah*, and many more *wallahs*; Malaysian English *botak head*; New Zealand English *sharemilker*; etc.), localized phraseologisms (e.g. Kenyan English *look at someone with bad eyes*, *break a leg* 'make pregnant without being married'), and localized construction types (e.g. Singaporean English *Can or not? – Can, lah!*). The Philippine English forms *to back-carry* and *to gift-give* are particularly interesting, since these are verbal compounds, a word formation type that is not productive in standard English (such forms are rare and only produced by backformation). Thus, the auto-organizing process has not just generated new individual formatives but actually expanded formation rules and constraints, added a new layer to network types. Growing levels of organizational complexity manifest themselves in various ways – for instance, in Cameroonian Pidgin in what Hoffmann (2022:16) calls the "'N belong N' construction," which is semantically transparent and productive: *gras bilong hed* 'grass belong head' = 'hair'; *wara bilong skin* 'water belong skin' = 'sweat', and so on. Some varieties, notably Caribbean creoles, create possessives by combining a prefix *fi* (derived from *for*) and personal pronouns (e.g. *fi-me* 'my'; eWAVE f17), or also by postnominal or even prenominal phrases (like *for my sister husband*) with *for*, with *bilong*, or with plain juxtaposition (eWAVE f74–77). Others build complex interrogatives by using additional formatives (*who-all*; eWAVE f39) or reduplication (*who-who*; eWAVE, f40). A low, possibly early manifestation of emerging chunking are observable co-occurrence tendencies, as for example in IndE, where *of which* tends to follow *as a result* more often than expected (Schneider 2020c:98). Vetchinnikova (2017) looks into chunking, lexical fixing in specific construction types and the formation of "lexical bundles," and argues that this is a process characteristic of emergence in CDSs. All these, and many more, are products of a language variety's self-organizing, emergent capacity.

Self-organization can also be taken to operate on more abstract levels, in the growth of new construction habits (function-form associations) in a speech community. Hoffmann (2014) hypothesizes that the emergence of mainly substantive constructions characterizes early phases of a new variety's evolution in the Dynamic Model, as opposed to "meso-constructional" schematic constructions which occur at later stages. In his 2021 Element he shows this to be true: Broadly, the more advanced varieties are in their developmental trajectory, the more creative and liberally lexically filled their schematic constructions are. Hoffmann (2021:21) calls this the "Dynamic Model Productivity hypothesis: Varieties in later phases of the Dynamic Model show (1) more productivity of the slots of (semi-) schematic construction than varieties in earlier developmental phases due to (2) less reliance on prototypical and frequent fillers."

World Englishes and Complex Dynamic System

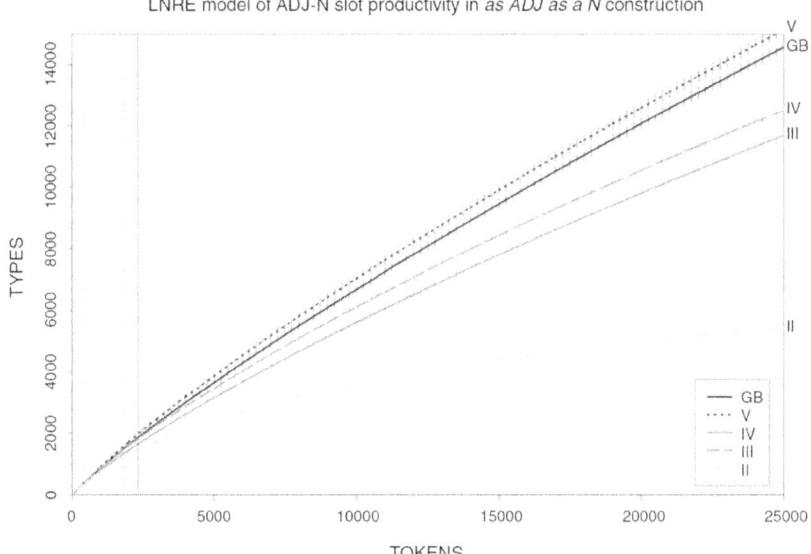

Figure 5 Productivity of the ADJ-N slots across Dynamic Model phases (Hoffmann 2021:45; CC-BY4.0 license)

To document this advanced type of productivity (equivalent to auto-emergence), Hoffmann (2022) employs "LNRE" ('Large Number of Rare Events') statistical models, and he shows that the hypothesis is basically valid, showing that self-organization shows the capacity of building abstract relations associated with variant forms in advanced network relations. Figure 5 shows a clear example. Based on several thousands of tokens from the well-known, monumental GloWbE corpus,[28] it shows the range of lexical variability in the "as ADJ as a N" construction, exemplified by *as quiet as a cemetery*, *as gentle as a lamb*, or *as fit as a fiddle*. The lines of the graph represent type-token ratios in varieties assigned to different phases of the Dynamic Model (plus GB, the erstwhile donor variety). All varieties show lexical variability of Adj-N pairs, increasingly so with higher token numbers. Most interestingly, however, it is perfectly clear that there is a strong correlation between productivity and Dynamic Model phases: "Phase V varieties show the highest productivity rate (even higher than the BrE reference variety), while Phase II varieties have the lowest productivity. Phase IV and Phase III can be found in between these two extremes (with Phase IV, however, significantly superseding Phase III varieties)" (Hoffmann 2022:45). Clearly, this can be seen as emergent grammar patterns and effects of self-organizing forces in the course of time.[29]

---

[28] www.english-corpora.org/glowbe/.
[29] Laporte (2021) offers similar findings with respect to abstract constructions involving the verb *make*.

Another example illustrating the same process, a simpler and less theoretically motivated one, is the expansion of ditransitives in IndE, shown by Mukherjee and Hoffmann (2006). Ditransitive constructions, with an indirect and a direct object (*I gave you a book*) are a common complementation pattern in English. As the authors documented, in IndE a much wider range of verbs allows this complementation pattern, thus building emergent schematic patterns and new networks between constructions and verbs (see Examples 5a–c).

(5) (a) the park would have provided the city the much-needed greenery
    (b) we presented each donor a travel bag
    (c) the FCI is not supplying us the foodgrain (all from Mukherjee & Hoffmann 2006)

Of course, various other constructions and examples discussed in other sections also illustrate the effects of auto-emergence in association with other CDS principles. For example, the distinctively Singlish construction with postponed relativizer *one* discussed in Section 4.3.2 (produced by "filtering" processes through Chinese impact; Bao 2015) can be taken to represent self-organization within this variety in association with network relations with other structures and with other substrate languages. Similarly, and interestingly, in some varieties the form *finish* has emerged as a marker of completeness of an activity (thus standing in paradigmatic network relation with the morphological past). This has been analyzed most thoroughly for children's English in Singapore (Buschfeld 2020, as in Examples 6a and 6b), but it is also documented for other high-contact varieties (e.g. Examples 6c and 6d).

(6) (a) He comb his hair finished.
    (b) She tie finish her shoe laces. (both Buschfeld 2020:202)
    (c) I cook finish. (Tok Pisin)
    (d) You finish eat? 'Have you eaten?' (Indian South African English; both quoted from Siemund 2013:119)

This usage of *finish* showcases a wide range of CDS properties: It has auto-emerged via self-organization (thus also showing ongoing change processes), operates systemically within past time reference options, increases the complexity of time reference options, and stands in network relations of various kinds, including the meaning of the word in English, input options and models from substrate languages (in Singapore Chinese V+*wán*-(*le*); Buschfeld 2020:201), and the grammatical options for time reference.

In fact, the domain of tense-modality-aspect expressions seems particularly liable to the self-organized, network-related emergence of newly grammaticalized uses in some varieties. This is illustrated by perfective *done* and remote-time *been* as auxiliaries in Earlier African American English (Schneider 1989:114–27) and some West African and Caribbean pidgins and creoles, or by innovative future time markers derived from English forms with other functions, as in *gwine* (Gullah), *busy* (White South African English), preverbal *go* (Nigerian Pidgin), or (derived from the adverbial *by-and-by*) *bae /bai* in Bislama and Tok Pisin (see Siemund 2013:121–22, 141). Compare also the wide range of innovative habitual marking strategies documented in WEs (eWAVE 90–93) or other distinctive patterns involving progressives or perfectives (e.g. eWAVE f89, 94–95, 97–98.

Another formative strategy found in several varieties that can be seen as auto-organizing is reduplication (or even multiple repetition of a single word) to express intensification or duration (see Examples 7a–c).

(7) (a) I walk-walk-walk 'I was walking' (Singapore)
  (b) Ay ben wed wed wed wed 'I waited for ages' (Kriol; both quoted from Siemund 2013:144)
  (c) fool-fool 'very foolish', small-small 'very small' (Jamaican Patwa), proper proper 'very properly', talk-talk 'discuss intensely', same same (widespread in Asia) (Schneider 2020a:113, 157, 215)

4.3.7 Nonlinearity and Fractals

As stated earlier, CDSs are best modeled mathematically by nonlinear equations, with exponents raised to higher powers than 1. It seems difficult to pin down this precise understanding of the notion in language, however, unless the commonly observed ups and downs of frequency changes of forms through time are metaphorically accepted as nonlinear. Given the central role of usage in the evolution of speech, ideally what we would need, and what would need to be modeled, is a complete record of all utterances made in a universe under investigation, and their quantitative relationship to speakers and contexts – but this is a thought experiment at best. Trivially, however, it is not difficult to posit and believe that nonlinearity, the absence of a proportional relation of changes between input and output, applies: clearly, the multitude of individuals involved, linguistic choices available, and possible situational settings is not connected by direct, linear functional relations, and is likely to produce nonlinear interactions, supported and possibly produced by the feedback loops in usage.

As stated earlier (in Section 2.2.7), nonlinear and fractal relations are therefore more difficult to identify and pin down in language evolution. Vetchinnikova (2017) assumes that the fractal nature of language manifests itself in "inherent similarity in shape" (279) across the social, structural and temporal dimensions (e.g. similarity between short-term and long-term changes, or similarities across idiolects [284]). Specifically, she views similarities in the patterns of chunking (multi-word unit patterning, e.g. the pattern "it is ADJ that" [289–97]) between the cognitive and the communal planes of language representation (which she postulates, observing similarities between fixing in an individual's language and the emergence of communal phraseological conventions [302]) as an indication of fractality. More broadly, the core processes of entrenchment and conventionalization postulated by Schmid (2020) can probably readily be viewed as fractal in nature – self-similar and emerging across manifestations at different levels of magnitude, from utterance type to conventionalized social settings to individuals, groups of speakers, and communities (and, on all levels of scale, associated utterances).

For regional and social variants of items in dialectology Kretzschmar (2009, 2015) most decidedly argued for and documented the fractal, scale-free nature of frequency distributions of tokens, stating: "The scale-free property of complex systems predicts that there will always be sub-populations at different scales" (Kretzschmar 2015:123). To put it more simply, irrespectively of how closely we zoom in, whether we consider a speech community, a large part or a small group of speakers in it, or an idiolect, the frequency relationship between alternative choices made will always be the same. He showed that the same frequency relationship, which he calls "A-curve" and is related to what he calls the "80/20 rule" in the business world, holds with respect to the variants of an item in his Linguistic Atlas data: Token frequency plots in a set of data often yield a small number of types with high token frequencies (the prototypical representatives of a category) as against a large number of rare alternatives (the "long tail"). Figure 6[30] shows this type of distribution for lexical variants of the concept 'thunderstorm,' based on frequency charts of items recorded in the *Linguistic Atlas of the Middle and South Atlantic States*: One item predominates strongly (*thunderstorm*, found 759 times), others trail it with moderate frequencies (*thundershower*, 248; *storm*, 136; *thundercloud*, 110), but very many other types (such as *squalls*, *rainstorms*, *blinger*, *hail storms*, etc.) occur but are offered extremely rarely, often only once. As Kretzschmar (2009, 2015) shows, the same type of distribution holds in a scale-free manner (i.e. independent of the magnitude and breadth of items represented, across subsets of subjects, and so on), and it is also found in other natural-language type-token relations such as frequencies of word collocates or of relativizer choices or construction types in text corpora (Kretzschmar 2015:94, 102–103). There is

---

[30] A very similar graph on CDSs in general, showing a scale-free, fractal-like, power-law distribution, is provided by Mitchell (2021:9.5).

World Englishes and Complex Dynamic System 61

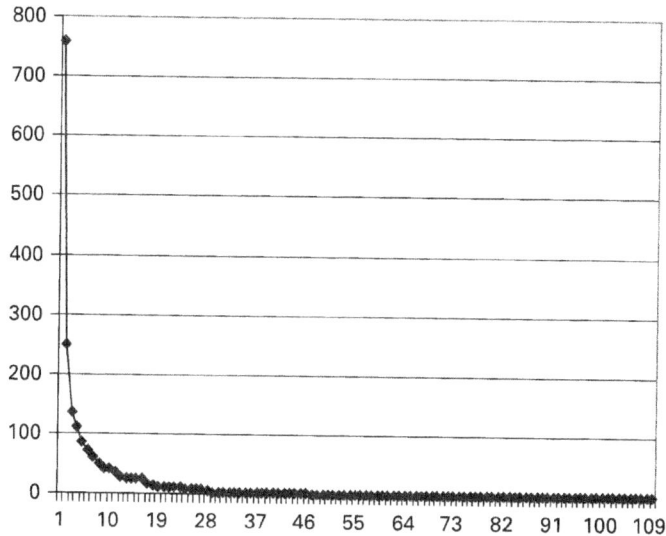

Figure 6 A-curve distribution of variants of 'thunderstorm' in LAMSAS (Kretzschmar 2009:98). Reproduced with permission of the Licensor through PLSclear.

always one or a small number of high-frequency predominant, prototypical form(s) in addition to a small set of intermediately frequent and many rare alternative choices. These distributions, he believes, are self-organizing patterns derived from neural network processes, a "sort of emergent order that we expect in language patterns from the operation of complex systems" (Kretzschmar 2015:147). Kretzschmar (2022) argues that the entire set of dialects (not to be reduced to the small set with conceptualized names) from all-encompassing "American English" down to any speaker group in between, independent of size and thus "scale," shows the same type of distribution. And, importantly, this fractal quantitative relationship holds the cradle of possible future change. He argues that any of the "great many variants in the long tail of the nonlinear frequency profile" (29) can become an "embryonic variant" which may spread in the community and ultimately result in systemic change.

This property of fractal, scale-free frequency distributions in language behavior is robust and well documented, and it is in line with another basic frequency distribution principle in language, Zipf's law (see Section 2.2.7). However, there is a limit to this observation: this type of distribution operates at certain dimensions, at several levels of magnitude (e.g. community, group, speaker) but not globally (unlike a fully fractal distribution like, for instance, the Mandelbrot set, where one can zoom in without limitations, with the pattern remaining the same).

Hence, in line with what was observed in Section 2.2.7, it seems meaningful to understand many frequency distributions in language as "fractal-like." Much of this has to do with the question of the level of granularity a researcher is aiming at – are we going for the "big picture" (focusing on frequent, mainstream phenomena), or are we interested in the observation and interpretation of small-scale variants and details? In this sense, a fractal perspective on WEs may also be implied in observing distributions across different levels of regional scale in varieties, given that, for example, there are several properties shared specifically across Asian Englishes (e.g. lack of articles), smaller-scale regional constellations (e.g., Malaysian and Singaporean English share the discourse marker *lah* and the *kena*-passive), particular variety types based on contact histories (Kortmann et al. 2020; Kortmann 2021), or simply properties of individual varieties (Schneider 2025b). Certainly, such similarities across several but not all magnitudes can be understood as quasi-fractal.[31]

4.3.8 Attractors

In second language acquisition, Larsen-Freeman (2018b) views learners' knowledge states as "attractors," modified by phase transitions and nonlinearity: "when the language resources of the learner change from one relatively stable attractor state to another, the point of transition is marked with increased behavioral variability, the result of nonlinearity. Having passed through a phase transition, the resources self-organize or restructure, where the new organization may be novel, qualitatively different from earlier organizations" (83; cf. Verspoor et al. 2008). In this sense "attractors" in the evolution of varieties can be understood as "preferred states" (Larsen-Freeman 2018a:52): usage habits or constructions that are easier to process, supported by frequency in discourse, or building mental associations and network relations to other, established, similar structures, backed by evident parallelisms.[32]

This "attracting" force, favoring one form of expression over another, can operate on several levels of complexity. In lexis, simple and transparent forms and those with high frequency will be preferred over rarer, internally complex or opaque lexemes. In Figure 7, spontaneously formed compounds like *working time* and *run time* are coined and preferred over a more idiomatic (but less well

---

[31] Such a looser understanding of the notion of scale seems in line with the fundamental discussion of the notion of Enfield (2023), who defines it somewhat vaguely as "the possibility for a measure to be larger or smaller in different instances of a system" (1).

[32] The German Linguistic Society (DGfS) announces a workshop "Attractors in Language Variation, Processing and Change" in 2025, suggesting "prominent linguistic elements" and favored patterns to which distributions are skewed as manifestations of attractors (LinguistList 35.2176).

Figure 7 Simplified lexical choices in China

Figure 8 Word class transfer (*lost* < *loss*) on Langkawi (Malaysia)

known) alternative *operating hours* because they are readily transparent, compositional for any reader. In Figure 8, a head noun (preceding *of properties*) is required, but we find what normally would be understood as a verb participle form (*lost of properties*) instead, presumably because the verb form is much more frequent,[33] thus more deeply entrenched and with an attracting force in a learner's usage-based body of English forms remembered. On a slightly more complex level, we find the same principle operating with some complementation patterns,

---

[33] For example, in COCA, the Corpus of Contemporary American English (www.english-corpora.org/coca/), there are about 220.000 tokens of *lost*, as opposed to 90.000 tokens of the noun *loss*).

for example "redundant" preposition choices as attractors. As is well known, in very many WEs the verb *discuss* takes not a direct object (as in metropolitan varieties: *discuss something*) but a preposition phrase with *about* (*discuss about something*; see Leuckert et al. 2023: section 5.3). This is clearly cross-motivated by the attractive force of the corresponding noun complementation (*a discussion about something*) and by the complementation of semantically very similar high-frequency verbs (*talk about something*), which thus invite cross-constructional mental associations. At the highest level of network complexity, we find schematic constructions which operate on the same formal and semantic associations as "attractors," taking variant lexical fillers, such as in the "way" construction: *donations find their way into the country*; *I . . . sleep my way to the top*; *we'll work our way through the Workbook* (Hoffmann 2021:33).

An interesting example from my own recent work is a study of the complementation of the multi-word verb *look forward to* (Schneider 2025a). Based on what originally was a coincidental, serendipitous observation which I then decided to trace systematically through several corpora from different countries and time periods, I found that the complementation of *look forward to* by a plain infinitive form rather than the verbal *-ing* participle called for in metropolitan varieties (*I look forward to meet you* rather than *to meeting you*) seems to have originated in IndE in the 1970s and to have spread and gained in frequency from there through decades: In IndE newspaper texts from the early 2000s as many as 40 percent of all verbal complementation patterns show this structure, with proportions only slightly lower in other sources, in other South Asian varieties, and, decreasing in frequency, in Southeast Asian and African ESL varieties. I argue that this is to be explained by the effect of second language acquisition processes, which favor simple, frequent, and transparent structures and may produce some degree of fossilization. In particular, the form *to*, which is homonymic with two completely different readings (a preposition, as in *to the holidays*, and an infinitive marker, as in *to go*), is primarily associated by learners with the infinitive function, which occurs about twice as often (in COCA) and is simpler (calling for a plain verb complement rather than a noun phrase or, in this case, a bimorphemic verbal *-ing* form), and it is also backed by (=associated with) other, formally and semantically similar structures such as *I hope to come*. Hence, the infinitive marking function of *to* in this construction apparently serves as an attractor to invite the plain infinitive complementation of *look forward to*, at the expense of the more complex "preposition + reduced *Ving* clause" reading.

A rather abstract and deeply rooted but consistently effective attractor seems to be a distinction originally discovered and documented by Mesthrie (2006).[34] Some

---

[34] On a more abstract, typological plane, this seems correspondent to the distinction between "recursive" and "condensatory" dimensions of language organisation (see Lund et al. 2022:viii).

NEs tend to delete many constituents that in mainstream grammar are considered mandatory. Take Example 8a, a typical utterance in Singlish: No subject, no lexical main verb, no further complements or constituents. In contrast, other varieties are characterized by what Mesthrie calls "anti-deletion": a tendency to restore features which are otherwise commonly deleted, such as the infinitive marker in Example 8b, to retain forms which are often deleted elsewhere (e.g. the complementizer *that* or a copula), and to insert additional grammatical morphemes (see Example 8c). Among other things, this corresponds to the "resumptive pronouns" identified by Siemund (2013:266–67; see Example 8d).

(8) (a) Can or not? – Can! (Singlish)
 (b) I let him to speak Zulu. (Black South African English; Mesthrie 2006:122)
 (c) As it is the case elsewhere, ... (Mesthrie 2006:127)
 (d) The guests whom I invited them have arrived (Nigerian English; Siemund 2013:266).

The "attractors" in his case are deeply rooted grammatical habits and associations, to be expressed as something like "Be maximally concise: avoid superfluous forms" in the case of the deleter varieties (mainly in Asia) as opposed to "Be maximally explicit: insert all possible forms to make the message clear" in anti-deletion varieties (primarily in Africa).

Again, the oscillation between "attractors" and the emergence of properties can be identified in association with other CDS principles, and thus with other examples discussed elsewhere in this Element. A case in point, for example, is the interplay between preferences for pre- or post-head positions of noun phrase modifiers in Asian versus African varieties discussed in Section 4.3.4. (Brunner 2017). The regionally predominant head-modifier sequences (e.g. Adj-N vs. N-Adj) as mentally entrenched preferred associations can be seen as constituting attractors, different ones in different world regions in this case. Similarly, the semantic force of the activity type readings associated with past tense and perfect forms, respectively, shaped in part by contextual conditions of migration and cross-varietal influences, can be regarded as attractors, with specific meanings intended calling for certain formal realizations, and, alternatively, forms chosen inviting particular temporal interpretations. The relative force of attraction in these cases varies by context and variety, and as we saw in Section 4.3.5, seems to have been diminishing in some NEs when compared to BrE.

5 Toward Agent-Based Modeling of Varieties Emergence Using NetLogo

Applications of CDS theory to real-life systemic relations typically employ one of three main methodological strategies. The most precise and most uncompromising mode of describing a system's behavior would be through modeling it mathematically with nonlinear equations. In reality, however, this is not so often practiced (and if so, then mostly in the hard sciences, where the interacting parameters are clearly defined and set), since the range of entities involved, the properties associated with them, and the processes operating between them are manifold, often huge, and fuzzy by their very nature, hence difficult to measure, categorize, and capture by means of mathematical tools. With regard to social and biological systems (like the growth of cities, the behavior of ant colonies, the operation of the blood system, etc.) it has been customary to argue for the operation of CDS principles somewhat metaphorically, as has been the case in this Element. Between these extreme options, the rigorous and the indirect one, as it were, there is a third that CDS theorists apply most widely, namely the modeling of CDS processes by computer simulations. Agent-based modeling simulation software gives the analyst the option of defining constituents as needed: agents and their heterogeneous properties, in large numbers; the parameters of a "world" (a two-dimensional plane, a three-dimensional cube, a network with customized nodes and links, or also, based on GIS software, geographical settings) in which the agents operate (move and exchange information, for example); rules as determined by the scientist, mirroring real-life relations and interactions. These interchanges between agents and their (possibly changing) properties in the "world" are normally visualized in appropriate ways, and the visualizations display step-by-step changes of systemic relations as defined by the rules, so that the evolution, operation and outcome of an evolving CDS become quite readily transparent and immediately observable.

The Santa Fe Institute, the globally leading research institution investigating CDSs, widely employs and recommends the freeware program NetLogo for such purposes (downloadable freely from http://ccl.northwestern.edu/netlogo). NetLogo is basically a programming language to simulate CDS behavior.[35] It consists of three interacting levels. First, code lines (written in a strictly defined syntax) define the world, the agents, their properties, relevant contextual parameters, and the rules of behavior and interaction. Secondly, NetLogo comes with a visualization panel (the "Interface," which can also be defined and customized as needed) which displays the evolutionary process and thus allows immediate insights into the emerging and changing systems. Thirdly, these two levels are accompanied by an associated natural-language description of the respective model (called "Info"), its assumptions, goals, and agents, and so on, to give an interested novice user an immediate idea of the goals,

---

[35] There are others as well, like Swarm, Repast, AScape, Mason, or mass. A toolkit that also implements "Fluid Construction Grammar," developed in Belgium, is Babel (https://emergent-languages.org/).

characteristics, parameters, and options of the respective model. "Setup" and "go" are basic commands which create a specific world state and get it moving and changing through a recursive sequence of (counted) evolutionary iterations (called "ticks"). By modifying the values of various pre-defined parameters (as qualitative choices modeled as switches or "choosers," or changing magnitudes through sliders) a user can "play with" the system, run it repeatedly and see which effects the changing parameters produce. NetLogo can assign properties to agents (and modify them based on predefined conditions), create links between agents (with specific properties and consequences), and introduce random effects. The program comes with a huge "Models Library" from many domains of life (Art, Biology, Chemistry, Earth Science, Philosophy, Psychology, Social Science, and so on), which can simply be chosen and opened, illustrating how the software works. Thus, for gaining initial familiarity with the operation of the software the initial learning curve is not steep (it is, though, later on, if a scientist wishes to devise models of their own).

The NetLogo Library contains a single application to language, a model called "Language Change," to be found under Social Science\Economics. The model shows two linguistic variants (generated by alternative grammars) competing with each other in a social network, with some individuals using a new grammatical form and others in their environment adopting it if certain conditions are met (e.g. if a certain proportion of neighbors uses the form in question). Relevant parameters (e.g. the number of nodes/individuals, the proportion of initial users of a given grammar form, threshold values for adoption) can be defined initially, and the visualization then shows how the innovation spreads after individual steps (ticks). Depending on initial settings, this model typically leads to either full adoption or disappearance of the innovative form after about 100 ticks (or so). Figure 9 illustrates the Language Change model in NetLogo, with the model (with given parameters) having run for 30 ticks and the innovative form shown as white dots.

Rand (2024:unit 4) develops a similar model (not in the library; final version available at https://s3.amazonaws.com/complexityexplorer/ABMwithNetLogo/model-7.nlogo) that simulates how novel information diffuses through a population over time – certainly closely related to the question of how a linguistic innovation spreads in a community. A user can define the number of agents, network types to choose from and their density, a threshold of adoption dependent on the amount of broadcast consumption and the number of other adopters, and a special agent type of "influentials" (as opposed to imitators) with their influence strength to be specified. Setting these parameters in varying ways then permits the generation and observation of different kinds and speeds of diffusion processes. Figure 10 presents an example of an intermediate state of this model, with adopters of the new information displayed in degrees of red.

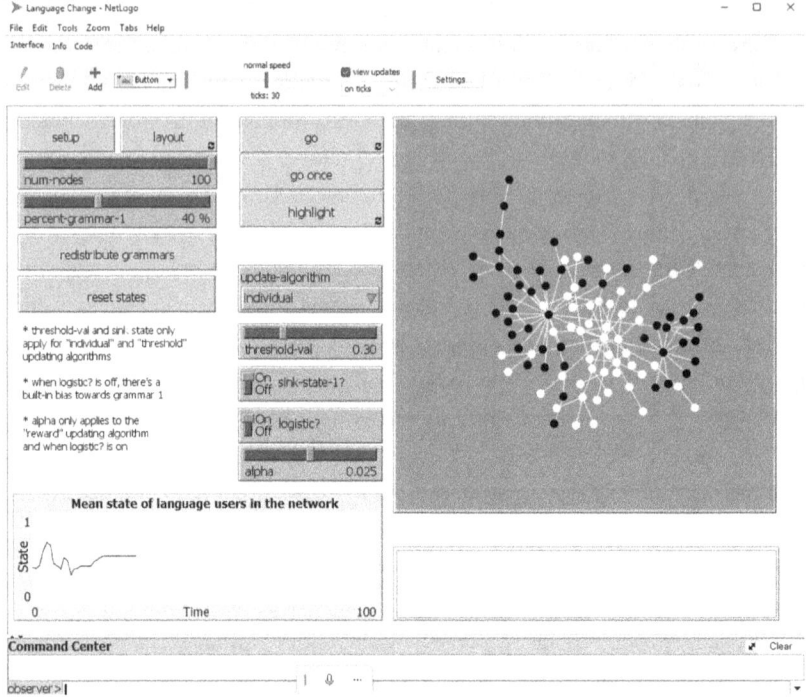

Figure 9 Example of a state of the "Language Change" model in NetLogo

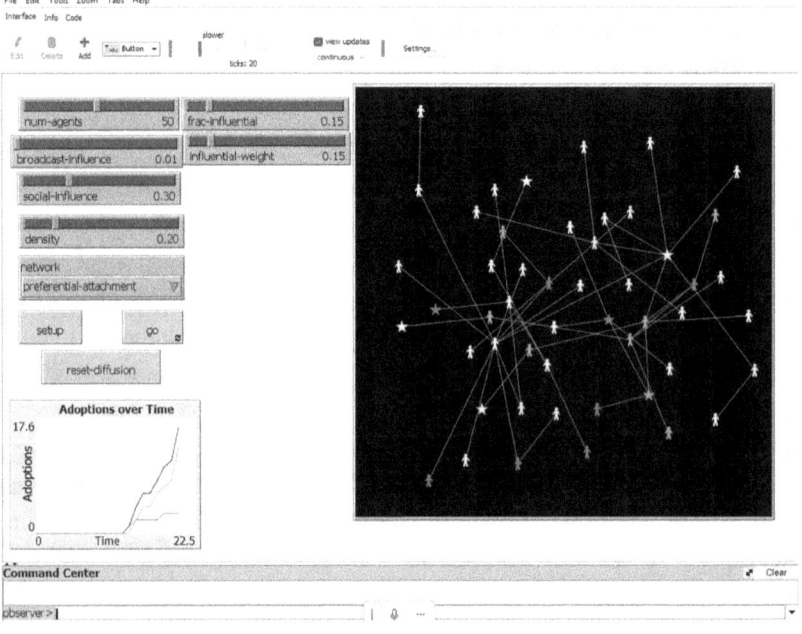

Figure 10 Example of a state of the new information diffusion model (Rand 2024:unit 4) in NetLogo

NetLogo can certainly be employed to simulate the emergence of varieties in similar ways,[36] for instance with distinctive innovative properties spreading only in part of the world, thus modeling the growth of individual varieties (or variety features). The world could be subdivided into two adjacent regions: partly overlapping networks (let's call them "nations") with a boundary and some transition points between them that reduces (but not completely prevents) the likelihood of an innovation being adopted by any single individual on the other side of the boundary. For reasons of space and technical sophistication (this would open a wholly new type of approach and mode of application, beyond the goal and character of this Element) this will not be pursued any further here, but I do think this option would be a fruitful direction for future research.[37]

6 Conclusion: World Englishes Keep Rolling

Given the arguments, examples, and evidence presented in this Element, it seems compelling that all Englishes constitute a CDS, and today's WEs, just like all other varieties, are components of it! They are marked by constant dynamism in interaction, the growth of complexity, the emergence of innovative structural relationships in specific contexts, and so on. This Element thus represents another call for a change of framework and perspective, toward a holistic and processual perspective rather than upholding a reductionist and segmenting, categorial view, in line with new tendencies in the sciences and the basic insight that the "reductionist approach is in a sense the opposite of what Complexity is all about" (Johnson 2009:17).

So, what have we gained? Is the adoption of this new CDS perspective in WEs research really a step forward? After all, CDS is a rather abstract, multifaceted perspective, not directly connected with conventional ways of thinking in linguistics. I am convinced it is: Like any useful theoretical framework it will help us understand better how language works and how varieties evolve, and it contributes to attributing respect and dignity to NEs and other emerging varieties. At this stage we need steps toward implementing this new perspective, building bridges between both ways of understanding Englishes.[38]

---

[36] I realize this section is somewhat different from the others in this Element, and it has basically no more than an informative and possibly suggestive character. Due to space limitations and the nature of my topic, this avenue of research is not pursued any further. I decided not to omit it, however, since I felt it important to show and plot a possible connection of my approach to work done by CDS scientists (at the Santa Fe Institute, for instance).

[37] The only application of this line of thinking that I am aware of is by Hundt and colleagues (2022), who use a program written in Python to model attitudes toward BrE and AmE in two speech communities, focusing on variant verb complementation choices and the concept of epicentral influence.

[38] Lund and colleagues (2022) claim that "it is no longer questioned that a complexity science framework is a useful way to conceptualize language use, acquisition, and change" (191).

Fundamentally, we need to be aware that applying CDS theory to WEs (or other varieties) constitutes an instance of modeling – the creation of a mirror image of reality that abstracts from some details to highlight those aspects and relations which are insightful and useful to foster understanding of something that in itself is difficult to grasp. As I stated elsewhere, in a rather different context, models are meant to be similar to reality and highlight important, useful properties (Schneider 2007:55, 57). Rand (2024) repeatedly quotes a pointed but insightful statement by George Box: "All models are wrong but some are useful." In CDS theory I have come across the best, most effective way of summarizing this slight dilemma: Jensen (2022:75–76; cf. ch. 4) quotes the "O'Keefe-Einstein propositions"(with the first attributed to the painter Georgia O'Keefe and the other two to Albert Einstein), phrased as follows:

(1) Nothing is less real than realism. Details are confusing. It is only by selection, by elimination, by emphasis, that we get at the real meaning of things.
(2) Make everything as simple as possible, but not simpler.
(3) A theory is the more impressive the greater simplicity of its premises, the more different kinds of things it relates, and the more extended its area of applicability.

Indirectly, these (or such) considerations and insights have motivated me to present these thoughts and claims concerning the relationship between CDS theory and WEs in particular. I realize these postulates open another can of worms, or many more, not to be addressed here and probably not to be solved by anyone in a principled way. But I do believe they neatly capture the essence of the relationship between World Englishes and Complex Dynamic Systems theory. CDS theory offers a new, more realistic perspective, perhaps a more convincing option to deviate from traditional prescriptive and categorial thinking. It is not meant to supersede earlier theories and models, since it operates on a broader level of scale, in a more fundamental perspective. Setting up categories for linguistic analysis is clearly helpful, and I am not arguing to do away with this established practice – but we should be aware of the fact that such concepts are heuristic devices, tools, also something like models – mirroring reality but also simplifying, reducing it, always abstracting from some (other) relevant, influential parameters.

I believe that the change of perspective advocated in this Element is particularly important in the field of WEs, where deeply engrained beliefs in the

---

Hopefully so, although I sense there is still a long way to go to see this perspective generally accepted; and to my knowledge it has not yet been applied to the field of WEs at all.

superiority of metropolitan Englishes (BrE and AmE) are still widely found in attitudes studies, and where there has always been a strong focus on "educated," formal and "correct" forms of the language, also as the target in language teaching. Against this established backdrop of a "standard lens" we need to recognize the importance of all the vibrant processes and communication practices on the ground, far from concerns about linguistic decorum or correctness. In reality we are ever so often confronted with natural acquisition of Englishes in context, "grassroots" emergence of forms of the language for specific purposes (Schneider 2016a; Meierkord & Schneider 2021), lingua franca uses, and language forms, bits and pieces of Englishes, being adopted as floating linguistic resources, independent of their origin (Pennycook 2007; Blommaert 2010; Meierkord 2012).

The CDS perspective can also shed a new, explanatory, and respectful light on structural properties (localized sound patterns, words, phraseology, or constructions) observed in WEs. So far many of these have been observed and described, and some have been explained as to their origins, often in contact phenomena. All too often, however, they have also been denigrated and branded as incorrect and not "proper English," and attitudes are widely critical and negative. Accounting for such patterns as products of CDS principles (as has been done in Section 4.3) suggests that such forms are legitimate products of principles of linguistic evolution, and manifestations of the creativity and productivity of their speakers.

Even more importantly, it needs to be emphasized that no single variety is intrinsically superior to any other – they all evolve through space and time, overlap more or less, keep changing, keep being affected by different network relations and attractor forces. Varieties may be diverging through space and time, but they are all fundamentally related with each other. It is uncontroversial that modern BrE and AmE and also their regional dialect variants (like northern English, Midwestern US English, etc.) are descendants of Old and Middle English after centuries of evolution. English itself is strongly a contact language (Schreier & Hundt 2013), however, and factoring in effects of migration and language contact in all kinds of settings has equally produced new varieties, new components of an ongoing CDS of Englishes. Braj Kachru, the main founding father of the field of WEs, consistently fought for the recognition of the legitimacy of "Outer Circle" and other varieties and their speakers' right to "ownership" of the language, and he was perfectly right in doing so. As stated at the end of Section 4.2, the CDS perspective highlights the important point in WE theorizing, often presented but by far not yet generally accepted, that all WEs are simply co-evolving varieties on equal footing. Varieties like IndE, Singaporean English, Cameroonian Pidgin, or Trinidadian Creole are equally legitimate descendants of Old English, just with different proportions and kinds of contact effects and emergent processes filtered in.

A consistent adoption of CDS thinking for World Englishes will thus return to and reinforce Kachru's original intention of assigning ownership to speakers of all varieties and of stating clearly that they are all on a par. It contributes to clarifying the fact that no single variety, neither BrE nor a New English, neither standard nor informal (nonstandard), is in any way superior or inferior to any other variety. Ontologically they are all of equal standing: They are all components of the overall CDS of Englishes, shaped by the same principles, undergoing the same processes, sharing some of the same associations, just indexically tied to different social settings and regions.

This Element, and Sections 4.3.1 to 4.3.8 in particular, have highlighted how evolutionary principles of CDS manifest themselves in the growth of World Englishes. Each in their own special ways these varieties build upon internal systemic relations, keep evolving perpetually, show network relations that contribute to existing complexity and increase it, often through self-organizing processes that may install or also disrupt orderly relations in partial subsystems, and sometimes display properties that can be seen as effects of nonlinearity, fractal organization, and the role of specific attractors. Of course, not all of these principles need to apply in every individual application case, and those that do interact in multiple ways. I am not arguing that WEs are particularly prone to being shaped by these principles and their effects; I chose them as a model case here because they constitute a coherent, widely studied varieties group with which I am thoroughly familiar, but in principle I assume that the same principles will operate with many other language varieties and languages in much the same way (and in a number of instances I showed that they worked in the history of English). Becoming aware of the role and the functioning of these principles is important, I firmly believe, because this will help us understand how language works, how this interacts with our human cognitive endowment, and that it is mistaken to assign varying intrinsic values (like being "good" or "bad," or right or wrong) to individual language forms and languages. Understanding evolution (and language and varieties evolution, for that matter) as an ongoing, complex, emergent process without value judgements associated with its components and products may help us to overcome boundaries and attitudes imposed by social hierarchies and differences. Creativity and versatility as embodied in the CDS principles are the spice of life, of the growth of languages, and also, boiled down to a more familiar scale, of the emergence of world Englishes.

References

Aarts, Bas. 1992. *Small Clauses in English: The Nonverbal Types*. Berlin: Mouton de Gruyter.

Adamou, Evangelia, & Yaron Matras. 2023. *The Routledge Handbook of Language Contact*. London: Routledge.

Aitchison, Jean. 2012. *Language Change: Progress or Decay?* 4th ed. Cambridge: Cambridge University Press.

Algeo, John. 2006. *British or American English? A Handbook of Word and Grammar Patterns*. Cambridge: Cambridge University Press.

Anderwald, Lieselotte. 2001. Was/were variation in non-standard British English today. *English World-Wide* 22, 1–22.

Archangeli, Diana, & Douglas Pulleyblank. 2022. *Emergent Phonology.* Berlin: Language Science Press.

Bao, Zhiming. 2015. *The Making of Vernacular Singapore English: System, Transfer and Filter*. Cambridge: Cambridge University Press.

Beckner, Clay, Richard Blythe, Joan Bybee, Morten H. Christiansen, William Croft, Nick C. Ellis, John Holland, Jinyun Ke, Diane Larsen-Freeman & Tom Schoenemann. 2009. Language is a complex adaptive system: Position paper. *Language learning* 59(s1), 1–26.

Bernaisch, Tobias. 2015. *The Lexis and Lexicogrammar of Sri Lankan English*. Amsterdam: John Benjamins.

Bernaisch, Tobias, & Claudia Lange. 2012. The typology of focus marking in South Asian Englishes. *Indian Linguistics* 73(1–4), 1–18.

Biermeier, Thomas. 2008. *Word-Formation in New Englishes: A Corpus-Based Analysis*. Berlin: Lit Verlag.

Blommaert, Jan. 2010. *The Sociolinguistics of Globalization*. Cambridge: Cambridge University Press.

Bossomaier, Terry. 2000. Complexity and neural networks. In Terry Bossomaier & David G. Green, eds., *Complex Systems*. Cambridge: Cambridge University Press, 367–406.

Bossomaier, Terry & David G. Green, eds. 2000. *Complex Systems*. Cambridge: Cambridge University Press.

Brown, Courtney. 1995. *Serpents in the Sand: Essays on the Nonlinear Nature of Politics and Human Destiny*. Ann Arbor: University of Michigan Press.

Brunner, Thomas. 2017. *Simplicity and Typological Effects in the Emergence of New Englishes*: *The Noun Phrase in Singaporean and Kenyan English*. Berlin: de Gruyter.

Buchanan, Mark. 2003. *Nexus: Small Worlds and the Groundbreaking Science of Networks*. New York: W. W. Norton.

Burkette, Allison, & William Kretzschmar. 2018. *Exploring Linguistic Science: Language Use, Complexity, and Interaction*. Cambridge: Cambridge University Press.

Buschfeld, Sarah. 2013. *English in Cyprus or Cyprus English? An Empirical Investigation of Variety Status*. Amsterdam: John Benjamins.

Buschfeld, Sarah. 2020. *Children's English in Singapore: Acquisition, Properties, and Use*. London: Routledge.

Buschfeld, Sarah, Thomas Hoffmann, Magnus Huber & Alexander Kautzsch, eds. 2014. *The Evolution of Englishes: The Dynamic Model and Beyond*. Amsterdam: John Benjamins.

Buschfeld, Sarah & Alexander Kautzsch. 2017. Towards an integrated approach to postcolonial and non-postcolonial Englishes. *World Englishes* 36, 104–26.

Buschfeld, Sarah & Alexander Kautzsch, eds. 2020. *Modelling World Englishes: A Joint Approach towards Postcolonial and Non-postcolonial Englishes*. Edinburgh: Edinburgh University Press.

Bybee, Joan. 2010. *Language, Usage and Cognition*. Cambridge: Cambridge University Press.

Bybee, Joan. 2015. *Language Change*. Cambridge: Cambridge University Press.

Canagarajah, A. Suresh. 2013. *Translingual Practice: Global Englishes and Cosmopolitan Relations*. London: Routledge.

Chambers, J.K. 2003. *Sociolinguistic Theory: Linguistic Variation and Its Social Significance*. Oxford: Blackwell.

Chambers, J.K. 2006–7. Geolinguistic patterns in a vast speech community. *Linguistica Atlantica* 27–28, 27–36.

Chambers, J.K., & Natalie Schilling, eds. 2013. *The Handbook of Language Variation and Change*. 2nd ed. Oxford: Blackwell.

Chernyshova, Elizaveta, Vanessa Piccoli & Biagio Ursi. 2022. Multimodal conversational routines: Talk-in-interaction through the prism of complexity. In Kristine Lund, Pierluigi Basso Fossali, Audrey Mazur & Magali Ollagnier-Beldame, eds., *Language Is a Complex Adaptive System: Explorations and Evidence*. Berlin: Language Science Press, 131–46.

Cheshire, Jenny. 1994. Standardization and the English irregular verbs. In Dieter Stein & Ingrid Tieken-Boon van Ostade, eds., *Towards a Standard English 1600–1800*. Berlin: Mouton de Gruyter, 115–33.

Christiansen, Morten, & Pablo Kontreras Callens. 2022. AI is changing scientists' understanding of language learning – and raising questions about an innate grammar. theconversation.com, 19 October. https://theconversation.com/ai-is-changing-scientists-understanding-of-language-learning-and-raising-questions-about-an-innate-grammar-190594.

Collins, Peter, & Xinyue Yao. 2012. Modals and quasi-modals in New Englishes. In Marianne Hundt & Ulrike Gut, eds., *Mapping Unity and Diversity World-Wide*. Amsterdam: John Benjamins, 35–53.

Cooper, David L. 1999. *Linguistic Attractors: The Cognitive Dynamics of Language Acquisition and Change*. Amsterdam: John Benjamins.

Croft, William. 2000. *Explaining Language Change*. Harlow: Longman.

de Bot, Kees. 2017. Complexity theory or dynamic systems theory: Same or different? In Lourdes Ortega & ZhaoHong Han, eds., *Complexity Theory and Language Development: In Celebration of Diane Larsen-Freeman*. Amsterdam: John Benjamins, 51–58.

de Bot, Kees, Wander Lowie & Marjolijn Verspoor. 2007. A dynamic systems theory approach to second language acquisition. *Bilingualism: Language and Cognition* 10, 7–21.

de Bot, Kees, HuiPing Chan, Wander Lowie, Rika Plat & Marjolijn Verspoor. 2012. A dynamic perspective on language processing and development. *Dutch Journal of Applied Linguistics* 1: 188–218.

Diaz-Campos, Manuel & Sonia Balasch, eds. 2023. *The Handbook of Usage-Based Linguistics*. Newark: Wiley & Sons.

Diessel, Holger. 2017. Usage-based linguistics. *Oxford Research Encyclopedia of Linguistics*. https://doi.org/10.1093/acrefore/9780199384655.013.363.

Du Bois, John. 1985. Competing motivations. In John Haiman, ed., *Iconicity in Syntax*. Amsterdam: John Benjamins, 343–65.

Edwards, Alison. 2016. *English in the Netherlands. Functions, Forms and Attitudes*. Amsterdam: John Benjamins.

Ellegård, Alvar. 1953. *The Auxiliary Do: the Establishment and Regulation of Its Use in English*. Stockholm: Almqvist & Wiksell.

Ellis, Nick C. 2008. The dynamics of second language emergence: cycles of language use, language change, and language acquisition. *The Modern Language Journal* 92, 233–49.

Ellis, Nick C. 2011. The emergence of language as a complex adaptive system. In James Simpson, ed., *The Routledge Handbook of Applied Linguistics*. London: Routledge, 666–79.

Ellis, Nick C., & Diane Larsen-Freeman, eds. 2009. *Language as a Complex Adaptive System*. Malden, MA: Wiley & Sons.

Enfield, Nick J. 2023. Scale in language. *Cognitive Science* 47, article e13341.

eWAVE: see Kortmann, Lunkenheimer & Ehret 2020.

Filppula, Markku, Juhani Klemola & Devyani Sharma, eds. 2017. *The Oxford Handbook of World Englishes*. Oxford: Oxford University Press.

Fischer, Olga, & Wim Van der Wurff. 2006. Syntax. In Richard Hogg & David Denison, eds., *A History of the English Language*. Cambridge: Cambridge University Press, 109–98.

Geeraerts, Dirk, & Hubert Cuyckens, eds. 2012. *The Oxford Handbook of Cognitive Linguistics*. Oxford: Oxford University Press.

Gerstner, Wulfram, Werner Kistler, Richard Naud & Liam Paninski. 2014. *Neuronal Dynamics: From Single Neurons to Networks and Models of Cognition*. Cambridge: Cambridge University Press.

Gibb, Sophie, Fobin Findlay Hendry, & Tom Lancaster, eds. 2019. *The Routledge Handbook of Emergence*. London: Routledge.

Goldberg, Adele E. 2006. *Constructions at Work: The Nature of Generalization in Language*. Oxford: Oxford University Press.

Görlach, Manfred. 1996. And is it English? *English World-Wide* 17, 153–74.

Green, David. 2000. Self-organisation in complex systems. In Terry Bossomaier & David G. Green, eds., *Complex Systems*. Cambridge: Cambridge University Press, 11–50.

Grund, Peter & Megan Hartman, eds., 2020. *Studies in the History of the English Language VIII: Boundaries and Boundary-Crossings in the History of English*. Berlin: Mouton de Gruyter.

Guastello, Stephen, Matthijs Koopmans & David Pincus, eds. 2009. *Chaos and Complexity in Psychology: The Theory of Nonlinear Dynamical Systems*. Cambridge: Cambridge University Press.

Guastello, Stephen, & Larry Liebovitch. 2009. Introduction to nonlinear dynamics and complexity. In Stephen Guastello, Matthijs Koopmans & David Pincus, eds., *Chaos and Complexity in Psychology: The Theory of Nonlinear Dynamical Systems*. Cambridge: Cambridge University Press, 1–40.

Gwee, Li Sui. 2018. *Spiaking Singlish: A Companion to How Singaporeans Communicate*. Singapore: Marshall Cavendish Editions.

Han, ZhaoHong. 2019. *Profiling Learner Language as a Dynamic System*. Bristol: Multilingual Matters.

Hansen, Beke. 2018. *Corpus Linguistics and Sociolinguistics: A Study of Variation and Change in the Modal Systems of World Englishes*. Leiden: Brill Rodopi.

Hickey, Raymond, ed. 2020. *Handbook of Language Contact*. 2nd ed. Malden: Blackwell.

Hilpert, Martin. 2013. *Constructional Change in English. Developments in Allomorphy, Word Formation, and Syntax*. Cambridge: Cambridge University Press.

Hilpert, Martin. 2019. *Construction Grammar and Its Application to English*. 2nd ed. Edinburgh: Edinburgh University Press.

Hiramoto, Mie, Wilkinson Daniel Wong Gonzales, Jakob Leimgruber, Lim Jun Jie & Jessica X. M. Choo. 2022. From Malay to Colloquial Singapore English: A case study of sentence-final particle *sia*. In Aloysius Ngefac, Hans-Georg Wolf & Thomas Hoffmann, eds., *World Englishes and Creole Languages Today. Vol. I: The Schneiderian Thinking and Beyond.* Munich: Lincom, 117–30.

Hiver, Phil, & Ali H. Al-Hoorie. 2019. *Research Methods for Complexity Theory in Applied Linguistics.* Bristol: Multilingual Matters.

Hoffmann, Thomas. 2014. The cognitive evolution of Englishes: The role of constructions in the Dynamic Model. In Sarah Buschfeld, Thomas Hoffmann, Magnus Huber & Alexander Kautzsch, eds., *The Evolution of Englishes: The Dynamic Model and Beyond.* Amsterdam: John Benjamins, 160–80.

Hoffmann, Thomas. 2019. *English Comparative Correlatives: Diachronic and Synchronic Variation at the Lexicon-Syntax Interface.* Cambridge: Cambridge University Press.

Hoffmann, Thomas. 2021. *The Cognitive Foundation of Post-colonial Englishes. Construction Grammar as the Cognitive Theory for the Dynamic Model.* Cambridge: Cambridge University Press.

Hoffmann, Thomas. 2022. *Construction Grammar: The Structure of English.* Cambridge: Cambridge University Press.

Hoffmann, Thomas, & Graeme Trousdale, eds. 2013. *The Oxford Handbook of Construction Grammar.* Oxford: Oxford University Press.

Holland, John H. 2014. *Complexity: A Very Short Introduction.* Oxford: Oxford University Press.

Hopper, Paul. 1987. Emergent grammar. *Berkeley Linguistics Society* 13, 139–57.

Hundt, Marianne, Laetitia Van Driessche & Dirk Pijpops. 2022. Epicentral influence via agent-based modelling. *World Englishes* 41, 377–99.

Jensen, Henrik Jeldtoft. 2022. *Complexity Science: The Study of Emergence.* Cambridge: Cambridge University Press.

Johnson, Neil. 2009. *Simply Complexity. A Clear Guide to Complexity Theory.* Oxford: Oneworld Publications.

Kachru, Braj B. 1985. Standards, codification and sociolinguistic realism: The English language in the outer circle. In Randolph Quirk & Henry G. Widdowson, eds., *English in the World: Teaching and Learning the Language and Literatures.* Cambridge: Cambridge University Press, 11–30.

Kachru, Braj B., ed. 1992. *The Other Tongue: English across Cultures.* 2nd ed. Chicago: University of Illinois Press.

Keller, Rudi. 1994. *On Language Change: The Invisible Hand in Language.* London: Routledge.

Koch, Christopher, Claudia Lange & Sven Leuckert. 2016. "This hair-style called as 'duck tail'": The 'intrusive *as*'-construction in South Asian varieties of English and Learner Englishes. *International Journal of Learner Corpus Research* 2, 151–76.

Kortmann, Bernd. 2021. Syntactic variation in English: A global perspective. In Bas Aarts, April McMahon & Lars Hinrichs, eds. *Handbook of English Linguistics*, 2nd ed. Hoboken, NJ: Wiley, 299–322.

Kortmann, Bernd, Kerstin Lunkenheimer & Katharina Ehret, eds. 2020. *The Electronic World Atlas of Varieties of English*. Zenodo. http://ewave-atlas.org.

Kortmann, Bernd & Edgar W. Schneider, in collaboration with Kate Burridge, Rajend Mesthrie & Clive Upton. 2004. *A Handbook of Varieties of English: A Multimedia Reference Tool*, 2 vols. Berlin: De Gruyter Mouton. https://doi.org/10.1515/9783110197181.

Kortmann, Bernd & Benedikt Szmrecsanyi. 2004. Global synopsis: Morphological and syntactic variation in English. In Bernd Kortmann, Edgar W. Schneider et al., eds., *A Handbook of Varieties of English: A Multimedia Reference Tool*, Vol. 2. Berlin: De Gruyter Mouton, 1142–202.

Kortmann, Bernd & Benedikt Szmrecsanyi, eds. 2012. *Linguistic Complexity: Second Language Acquisition, Indigenization, Contact*. Berlin: Mouton de Gruyter.

Krakauer, David. 2023. What is complexity? www.youtube.com/watch?v=FBkFu1g5PlE.

Kretzschmar, William R., Jr. 2009. *The Linguistics of Speech*. Cambridge: Cambridge University Press.

Kretzschmar, William R., Jr. 2014. Emergence of 'New Varieties' in speech as a complex system. In Sarah Buschfeld, Thomas Hoffmann, Magnus Huber & Alexander Kautzsch, eds., *The Evolution of Englishes: The Dynamic Model and Beyond*. Amsterdam: John Benjamins, 142–59.

Kretzschmar, William R., Jr. 2015. *Language and Complex Systems*. Cambridge: Cambridge University Press.

Kretzschmar, William R., Jr. 2022. The emergence of new varieties of English in North America: complex systems. In Merja Kytö & Lucia Siebers, eds., *Earlier North American Englishes*. Amsterdam: John Benjamins, 21–36.

Kroch, Anthony. 1989. Reflexes of grammar in patterns of language change. *Language Variation and Change* 1, 199–244.

Krug, Manfred. 2000. *Emerging English Modals: A Corpus-Based Study of Grammaticalization*. Berlin: Mouton de Gruyter.

Labov, William, 1994. *Principles of Linguistic Change*. Vol. 1: *Internal Factors*. Oxford: Blackwell.

Lange, Claudia. 2012. *The Syntax of Spoken Indian English*. Amsterdam: John Benjamins.

Lange, Claudia. 2016. The 'intrusive *as*'-construction in South Asian varieties of English. *World Englishes* 35, 133–46.

Laporte, Samantha. 2021. *Corpora, Constructions, New Englishes: A Constructional and Variationist Approach to Verb Patterning*. Amsterdam: John Benjamins.

Larsen-Freeman, Diane. 1997. Chaos/complexity science and second language acquisition. *Applied Linguistics* 18, 141–65.

Larsen-Freeman, Diane. 2017. Complexity theory: The lessons continue. In Lourdes Ortega & ZhaoHong Han, eds., *Complexity Theory and Language Development: In Celebration of Diane Larsen-Freeman*. Amsterdam: John Benjamins, 11–50.

Larsen-Freeman, Diane. 2018a. Complexity and ELF. In Jennifer Jenkins, W. Baker & Martin Dewey, eds. *The Routledge Handbook of English as a Lingua Franca*. Abington: Routledge, 51–60.

Larsen-Freeman, Diane. 2018b. Second language acquisition, WE, and language as a complex adaptive system (CAS). *World Englishes* 37, 80–92.

Larsen-Freeman, Diane & Lynne Cameron. 2008. *Complex Systems and Applied Linguistics*. Oxford: Oxford University Press.

Leuckert, Sven, Claudia Lange, Tobias Bernaisch & Asya Yurchenko. 2023. *Indian Englishes in the Twenty-First Century: Unity and Diversity in Lexicon and Morphosyntax*. Cambridge: Cambridge University Press.

Lightfoot, David. 1979. *Principles of Diachronic Syntax*. Cambridge: Cambridge University Press.

Lightfoot, David. 1991. *How to Set Parameters: Arguments from Language Change*. Cambridge, MA: MIT Press.

Lim, Lisa. 2004. *Singapore English. A Grammatical Description*. Amsterdam: John Benjamins.

Lim, Lisa. 2007. Mergers and acquisitions: On the ages and origins of Singapore English particles. *World Englishes* 26, 446–73.

Lindblom, Björn, Peter MacNeilage & Michael Studdert-Kennedy. 1984. Self-organizing processes and the explanation of language universals. In Brian Butterworth, Bernard Comrie & Östen Dahl, eds., *Explanations for Language Universals*. Berlin: de Gruyter, 181–203.

Lund, Kristine, Pierluigi Basso Fossali, Audrey Mazur & Magali Ollagnier-Beldame, eds. 2022. *Language Is a Complex Adaptive System: Explorations and Evidence*. Berlin: Language Science Press.

Mair, Christian. 2013. The world system of Englishes: Accounting for the transnational importance of mobile and mediated vernaculars. *English World-Wide* 34, 253–78.

Massip-Bonet, Àngels. 2019. Linguistic variation and change: Approach from the perspective of Complex Adaptive Systems. In Àngels Massip-Bonet, Gemma Bel-Enguix & Albert Bastardas-Boada, eds., *Complexity Applications in Language and Communication Sciences*. Cham: Springer, 77–92.

Massip-Bonet, Àngels, Gemma Bel-Enguix & Albert Bastardas-Boada, eds., 2019. *Complexity Applications in Language and Communication Sciences*. Cham: Springer.

Matras, Yaron. 2020. *Language Contact*. 2nd ed. Cambridge: Cambridge University Press.

Mauranen, Anna. 2017. A glimpse of ELF. In Markku Filppula, Juhani Klemola, Anna Mauranen & Svetlana Vetchinnikova, eds., *Changing English: Global and Local Perspectives*. Berlin: Mouton de Gruyter, 223–53.

Mauranen, Anna. 2018. Conceptualising ELF. In Jennifer Jenkins, Will Baker & Martin Dewey, eds., *The Routledge Handbook of English as a Lingua Franca*. London: Routledge, 7–24.

McArthur, Tom. 1998. *The English Languages*. Cambridge: Cambridge University Press.

McArthur, Tom. 2002. *Oxford Guide to World English*. Oxford: Oxford University Press.

McColl Millar, Robert. 2000. *System Collapse, System Rebirth: The Demonstrative Pronouns of English 900–1350 and the Birth of the Definite Article*. Oxford: Peter Lang.

Mehrotra, Raja Ram. 1998. *Indian English: Texts and Interpretation*. Amsterdam: John Benjamins.

Meierkord, Christiane. 2012. *Interactions across Englishes: Linguistic Choices in Local and International Contact Situations*. Cambridge: Cambridge University Press.

Meierkord, Christiane, & Edgar W. Schneider, eds. 2021. *World Englishes at the Grassroots*. Edinburgh: Edinburgh University Press.

Mesthrie, Rajend. 2006. Anti-deletions in an L2 grammar: A study of Black South African English mesolect. *English World-Wide* 27, 111–45.

Mesthrie, Rajend, & Rakesh Bhatt. 2008. *World Englishes*. Cambridge: Cambridge University Press.

Miestamo, M., K. Sinnemäki, & F. Karlsson, eds. 2008. *Language Complexity: Typology, Contact, Change*. Amsterdam: John Benjamins.

Milroy, Leslie. 1980. *Language and Social Networks*. Oxford: Blackwell.

Minelli, Tullio. 2009. Neurodynamics and electrocortical activity. In Guastello, Stephen, Matthijs Koopmans & David Pincus, eds. *Chaos and Complexity in Psychology: The Theory of Nonlinear Dynamical Systems*. Cambridge: Cambridge University Press, 73–107.

Mitchell, Melanie. 2021. Introduction to complexity. www.complexityexplorer.org/courses/119-introduction-to-complexity-2021

Mobus, George E., & Michael C. Kalton. 2015. *Principles of Systems Science*. New York: Springer.

Mufwene, Salikoko S. 2001. *The Ecology of Language Evolution*. Cambridge: Cambridge University Press.

Mufwene, Salikoko S. 2008. *Language Evolution. Contact, Competition and Change*. London: continuum.

Mufwene, Salikoko S., Christophe Coupé & Francois Pellegrino. 2017. *Complexity in Language: Developmental and Evolutionary Perspectives*. Cambridge: Cambridge University Press.

Mufwene, Salikoko S., & Anna Maria Escobar, eds. 2022. *The Cambridge Handbook of Language Contact*. 2 vols. Cambridge: Cambridge University Press.

Mukherjee, Joybrato, & Sebastian Hoffmann. 2006. Describing verb-complementational profiles of New Englishes. A pilot study of Indian English. *English World-Wide* 27, 147–73.

Mukherjee, Joybrato, & Marianne Hundt. 2011. *Exploring Second-Language Varieties of English and Learner Englishes: Bridging the Paradigm Gap*. Amsterdam: John Benjamins.

Nelson, Cecil, Zoya Proshina & Daniel Davis, eds. 2020. *The Handbook of World Englishes*. 2nd ed. Malden: Blackwell.

Nevalainen, Terttu. 2015. Descriptive adequacy of the S-curve model in diachronic studies of language change. In Christina Sanchez-Stockhammer, ed., *Can We Predict Linguistic Change?* Studies in Variation, Contacts and Change in English 16. www.helsinki.fi/varieng/series/volumes/16/

Newmeyer, Frederick & Laurel B. Preston, eds. 2014. *Measuring Grammatical Complexity*. Oxford: Oxford University Press.

Ortega, Lourdes, & ZhaoHong Han. 2017. *Complexity Theory and Language Development: In Celebration of Diane Larsen-Freeman*. Amsterdam: John Benjamins.

Pennycook, Alastair. 2007. *Global Englishes and Transcultural Flows*. London: Routledge.

Quirk, Randolph, Sidney Greenbaum, Geoffrey Leech, & Jan Svartvik. 1985. *A Comprehensive Grammar of the English Language*. London: Longman.

Rand, William. 2024. An introduction to agent-based modelling. www.complexityexplorer.org/courses/183-introduction-to-agent-based-modeling/

Rissanen, Matti. 1997. The pronominalization of *one*. In Matti Rissanen, Merja Kytö & Kirsi Heikkonen, eds., *Grammaticalization at Work. Studies of Long-term Developments in English*. Berlin: Mouton de Gruyter, 87–143.

Rüdiger, Sofia. 2019. *Morpho-Syntactic Patterns in Spoken Korean English*. Amsterdam: John Benjamins.

Rüdiger, Sofia, & Alex Baratta. 2025. *Transnational Korean Englishes*. Cambridge: Cambridge University Press.

Sailaja, Pingali. 2009. *Indian English*. Edinburgh: Edinburgh University Press.

Sampson, G. R., David Gil, & Peter Trudgill, eds. 2009. *Language Complexity as an Evolving Variable*. Oxford: Oxford University Press.

Sapir, Edward. 1921. *Language*. New York: Harcourt & Brace.

Saussure, Ferdinand de. 2016. *Cours de linguistique générale*. Paris: Payot.

Schmid, Hans–Jörg. 2020. *The Dynamics of the Linguistic System*. Oxford: Oxford University Press.

Schneider, Edgar W. 1989. *American Earlier Black English. Morphological and Syntactic Variables*. Tuscaloosa: University of Alabama Press.

Schneider, Edgar W. 1997a. Chaos theory as a model for dialect variability and change? In Alan R. Thomas, ed., *Issues and Methods in Dialectology*. Bangor: Department of Linguistics, University of Wales, 22–36.

Schneider, Edgar W. 1997b. *As* as 'is'. Is *as* 'is'?" In Udo Fries, Viviane Müller & Peter Schneider, eds., *From Aelfric to the New York Times: Studies in English Corpus Linguistics: Festschrift for Gunnel Tottie*. Amsterdam: Rodopi, 33–50.

Schneider, Edgar W. 2003. The dynamics of New Englishes: From identity construction to dialect birth. *Language* 79, 233–81.

Schneider, Edgar W. 2007. *Postcolonial English: Varieties Around the World*. Cambridge: Cambridge University Press.

Schneider, Edgar W. 2011. English into Asia: From Singaporean ubiquity to Chinese learners' features. In Anne Curzan & Michael Adams, eds., *Contours of English and English Language Studies: In Honor of Richard W. Bailey*. Ann Arbor: University of Michigan Press, 135–56.

Schneider, Edgar W. 2014. New reflections on the evolutionary dynamics of World Englishes. *World Englishes* 33, 9–32.

Schneider, Edgar W. 2016a. Grassroots Englishes in tourism interactions. *English Today* 32(3), 2–10.

Schneider, Edgar W. 2016b. Hybrid Englishes: An exploratory survey. *World Englishes* 35, 339–54.

Schneider, Edgar W. 2020a. *English Around the World. An Introduction.* 2nd ed. Cambridge: Cambridge University Press.

Schneider, Edgar W. 2020b. *Calling* Englishes *as* Complex Dynamic Systems: diffusion and restructuring. In Anna Mauranen & Svetlana Vetchinnikova, eds., *Language Change: The Impact of English as a Lingua Franca.* Cambridge: Cambridge University Press, 15–43.

Schneider, Edgar W. 2020c. Meanderings from early English to World Englishes: A Complex Systems perspective on morphosyntactic changes in *wh*-pronouns. In Peter Grund & Megan Hartman, eds., Studies in the History of the English Language VIII: *Boundaries and Boundary-Crossings in the History of English.* Berlin: Mouton de Gruyter, 73–105.

Schneider, Edgar W. 2023. The role of prescriptivism in the emergence of New Englishes. In Joan C. Beal, Morana Lukač & Robin Straaijer, eds., *The Routledge Handbook of Linguistic Prescriptivism.* London: Routledge, 103–20.

Schneider, Edgar W. 2025a. *Looking forward to meet you*: an embryonic pattern in Asian Englishes? In Adam Smith, Peter Collins & Minna Korhonen, eds. *World-wide Perspectives on English Usage: Into the Third Millennium.* Cambridge: Cambridge University Press.

Schneider, Edgar W. 2025b. Pluricentricity versus pluriareality? Areal patterns in the English-speaking world. In Ryan Durgasingh & Philipp Meer, eds., *Pluricentricity and Pluriareality: Dialects, Variation, and Standards.* Amsterdam: John Benjamins, 90–117.

Schneider, Edgar W. & Sarah Buschfeld. 2020. Expanding boundaries of a function word: uses of *one* in Early Modern and Modern English. In Peter Grund & Megan Hartman, eds., *Studies in the History of the English Language VIII: Boundaries and Boundary-Crossings in the History of English.* Berlin: Mouton de Gruyter, 135–66.

Schreier, Daniel. 2005. *Consonant Change in English Worldwide: Synchrony Meets Diachrony.* New York: Palgrave Macmillan.

Schreier, Daniel & Marianne Hundt, eds. 2013. *English as a Contact Language.* Cambridge: Cambridge University Press.

Schreier, Daniel, Marianne Hundt & Edgar W. Schneider, eds. 2020. *The Cambridge Handbook of World Englishes.* Cambridge: Cambridge University Press.

Schröder, Anne, ed. 2021. *The Dynamics of English in Namibia.* Amsterdam: John Benjamins.

Schumann, John H. 2017. Neural complexity meets lexical complexity. An issue in both language and in neuroscience. In Lourdes Ortega & ZhaoHong Han, *Complexity Theory and Language Development: In Celebration of Diane Larsen-Freeman.* Amsterdam: John Benjamins, 59–78.

Seargeant, Philip & Caroline Tagg. 2011. English on the internet and a 'post-varieties' approach to language. *World Englishes* 30, 496–514.

Seeley, D. A. 2000. Network evolution and the emergence of structure. In Terry Bossomaier, & David G. Green, eds., *Complex Systems*. Cambridge: Cambridge University Press, 51–89.

Siemund, Peter. 2013. *Varieties of English: A Typological Approach*. Cambridge: Cambridge University Press.

Stenroos, Merja. 2008. Order out of chaos? The English gender change in the Southwest Midlands as a process of semantically based reorganization. *English Language and Linguistics* 12, 445–73.

Tamaredo, Iván. 2020. *Complexity, Efficiency, and Language Contact: Pronoun Omission in World Englishes*. Bern: Peter Lang.

Thomason, Sarah G. 2001. *Language Contact: An Introduction*. Washington, DC: Georgetown University Press.

Thomason, Sarah Grey, & Terrence Kaufman. 1988. *Language Contact, Creolization, and Genetic Linguistics*. Berkeley: University of California Press.

Tomasello, Michael. 2003. *Constructing a Language: A Usage-Based Theory of Language Acquisition*. Cambridge, London: Harvard University Press.

Trudgill, Peter. 2011. *Sociolinguistic Typology: Social Determinants of Linguistic Complexity*. Oxford: Oxford University Press.

Ungerer, Tobias, & Stefan Hartmann. 2023. *Constructionist Approaches. Past, Present, Future*. Cambridge: Cambridge University Press.

Verspoor, Marjolijn, Wander Lowie & Marijn van Dijk. 2008. Variability in second language development from a dynamic systems perspective. *The Modern Language Journal* 92, 214–31.

Verspoor, Marjolijn. 2012. Symposium: Dynamic systems/Complexity theory as a new approach to second language development. *Language Teaching* 45, 533–34.

Vetchinnikova, Svetlana. 2017. On the relationship between the cognitive and the communal: a complex systems perspective. In Markku Filppula, Juhani Klemola, Anna Mauranen & Svetlana Vetchinnikova, eds., *Changing English. Global and Local Perspectives*. Berlin, Boston: Mouton de Gruyter, 277–310.

Wee, Lionel. 2003. The birth of a particle: *know* in Colloquial Singapore English. *World Englishes* 34, 5–13.

Werner, Valentin. 2014. *The Present Perfect in World Englishes: Charting Unity and Diversity*. Bamberg: University of Bamberg Press.

Werner, Valentin, Elena Seoane, & Cristina Suárez-Gómez, eds. 2016. *Reassessing the Present Perfect*. Berlin: de Gruyter.

Winford, Donald. 2003. *An Introduction to Contact Linguistics*. Oxford: Blackwell.
Wolfram, Walt, & Natalie Schilling-Estes. 1997. *Hoi Toide on the Outer Banks*. Chapel Hill: University of North Carolina Press.
Xu Wen & John R. Taylor, eds. 2021. *The Routledge Handbook of Cognitive Linguistics*. New York: Routledge.

Acknowledgments

I would like to thank Isabel Collins for organizing the reviewing process of this Element, and two anonymous reviewers for their thorough reading and their helpful and insightful comments.

For Cleo, my little sunshine,
who somehow embodies all the principles discussed here ☺

World Englishes

Edgar W. Schneider
University of Regensburg

Edgar W. Schneider is Professor Emeritus of English Linguistics at the University of Regensburg, Germany. His many books include *Postcolonial English* (Cambridge, 2007), *English around the World*, 2e (Cambridge, 2020) and *The Cambridge Handbook of World Englishes* (Cambridge, 2020).

Editorial Board

Alexandra D'Arcy, *University of Victoria*
Kate Burridge, *Monash University*
Paul Kerswill, *University of York*
Christian Mair, *University of Freiburg*
Christiane Meierkord, *Ruhr University*
Raj Mesthrie, *University of Cape Town*
Miriam Meyerhoff, *Victoria University of Wellington*
Daniel Schreier, *University of Zurich*
Devyani Sharma, *Queen Mary University of London*
Sali Tagliamonte, *University of Toronto*
Bertus van Rooy, *University of Amsterdam*
Lionel Wee, *National University of Singapore*

About the Series

Over the last centuries, the English language has spread all over the globe due to a multitude of factors including colonization and globalization. In investigating these phenomena, the vibrant linguistic sub-discipline of "World Englishes" has grown substantially, developing appropriate theoretical frameworks and considering applied issues. This Elements series will cover all the topics of the discipline in an accessible fashion and will be supplemented by on-line material.

Cambridge Elements

World Englishes

Elements in the Series

Uniformity and Variability in the Indian English Accent
Caroline R. Wiltshire

Posthumanist World Englishes
Lionel Wee

The Cognitive Foundation of Post-colonial Englishes: Construction Grammar as the Cognitive Theory for the Dynamic Model
Thomas Hoffmann

Inheritance and Innovation in the Evolution of Rural African American English
Guy Bailey, Patricia Cukor-Avila and Juan Salinas

Indian Englishes in the Twenty-First Century: Unity and Diversity in Lexicon and Morphosyntax
Sven Leuckert, Claudia Lange, Tobias Bernaisch and Asya Yurchenko

Language Ideologies and Identities on Facebook and TikTok: A Southern Caribbean Perspective
Guyanne Wilson

Transnational Korean Englishes
Sofia Rüdiger and Alex Baratta

Multiscriptal English in Transliterated Linguistic Landscapes
Chonglong Gu

World Englishes as Components of a Complex Dynamic System
Edgar W. Schneider

A full series listing is available at: www.cambridge.org/EIWE

For EU product safety concerns, contact us at Calle de José Abascal, 56–1°,
28003 Madrid, Spain or eugpsr@cambridge.org.

www.ingramcontent.com/pod-product-compliance
Lightning Source LLC
LaVergne TN
LVHW011851060526
838200LV00054B/4277